PROSPERITY:
Is It by Law or Grace?

STEWART ROBERTSON

BALBOA.
PRESS

A DIVISION OF HAY HOUSE

Scripture taken from the New King James Version®. Copyright © 1982 by Thomas Nelson. Used by permission. All rights reserved.

Scripture quotations marked (KJV) are taken from the King James Version.

Scripture quotations are taken from the Holy Bible, New Living Translation, copyright ©1996, 2004, 2007, 2013, 2015 by Tyndale House Foundation. Used by permission of Tyndale House Publishers, Inc., Carol Stream, Illinois 60188. All rights reserved.

Scripture quotations marked HCSB are taken from the Holman Christian Standard Bible®, Used by Permission HCSB ©1999,2000,2002,2003,2009 Holman Bible Publishers. Holman Christian Standard Bible®, Holman CSB®, and HCSB® are federally registered trademarks of Holman Bible Publishers.

Balboa Press books may be ordered through booksellers or by contacting:

Balboa Press
A Division of Hay House
1663 Liberty Drive
Bloomington, IN 47403
www.balboapress.com.au
1 (877) 407-4847

Because of the dynamic nature of the Internet, any web addresses or links contained in this book may have changed since publication and may no longer be valid. The views expressed in this work are solely those of the author and do not necessarily reflect the views of the publisher, and the publisher hereby disclaims any responsibility for them.

The author of this book does not dispense medical advice or prescribe the use of any technique as a form of treatment for physical, emotional, or medical problems without the advice of a physician, either directly or indirectly. The intent of the author is only to offer information of a general nature to help you in your quest for emotional and spiritual well-being. In the event you use any of the information in this book for yourself, which is your constitutional right, the author and the publisher assume no responsibility for your actions.

Any people depicted in stock imagery provided by Thinkstock are models, and such images are being used for illustrative purposes only.
Certain stock imagery © Thinkstock.

Print information available on the last page.

ISBN: 978-1-5043-0657-7 (sc)
ISBN: 978-1-5043-0658-4 (e)

Balboa Press rev. date: 02/07/2017

CONTENTS

Acknowledgements...vii
Foreword..ix
Introduction...xi

Part 1
Old Testament, Old Covenant 1

Part 2
Grace: The New Covenant..32

Part 3
The Global Financial System..78

Part 4
Personal Prosperity... 114

Part 5
Excellent Health... 169

Part 6
Kingdom Living... 236

References... 253

ACKNOWLEDGEMENTS

My wife, Merilyn, and I celebrated our forty-first wedding anniversary on 15 November 2016. Merilyn has been a wonderful help, painstakingly going through this manuscript and being my proofreader, editor, and typist.

I also wish to express my profound thanks to Magdalena, who was the second person God told that I was going to write a book. I absolutely knew that I was being directed by God to write this timely book in these most uncertain times. It is my sincere prayer that many people will be healed and have an abundant fulfilling life as they get to know the living Saviour, the Lord Jesus Christ, who is the author and finisher of our faith.

FOREWORD

I believe that every person who reads this book, whether believer or nonbeliever, will know that these are life principles by which to live. From the beginning, almighty God gave us commandments and instructions throughout His word, the Bible, about avoiding debt, sowing into His kingdom, sustaining our bodies by treating them as temples, and loving each other. This book brings us back to the very fundamentals of living life as our maker intended.

This is a must-read. Everyone reading this foreword should get the book; they will learn through every page that God gave us basic principles to live by to simplify our journey on earth. By sustaining every portion given to you, you can prosper, adjust your way of thinking, and change your circumstances to become blessed and to be a blessing to others.

I am so privileged to have been asked by my dear friend, Stewart, to write the foreword to his book. I believe both Stewart and his precious wife, Merilyn, are led by the Holy Spirit in everything they do. Every chapter in this book is backed up by scripture, and all scripture is only truth. I know you will be blessed.

Tracey Verwey
Prophet to the Nations

INTRODUCTION

Why Prosperity?

You may be wondering, why another book on prosperity? We already have a plethora of books on the subject. I have noticed, in my forty-five years as a Christian, a large number of Christians seem to be struggling, even though they are trying to follow a formula that will give them financial success.

Remember: When we take a detailed examination of this subject, we must take the scriptures literally unless it is clearly figurative, for example Matthew 18:9 (NKJV). (Most citations are from the NKJV unless otherwise stated eg. HSCB).

"And if your eye causes you to sin, pluck it out and cast it from you. It is better for you to enter into life with one eye, rather than having two eyes, to be cast into hell fire."

Jesus is not telling you to pluck out your physical eye, but to be extremely careful what you let your eyes dwell on. Secondly, do not spiritualise a literal passage to make it fit into your church traditions; this will be explained in more detail in the coming chapters.

How did I know that almighty God, omniscient (all-knowing) Holy Spirit, wanted me to write this book? In 2013, I was at a men's breakfast, and a man I had only just met said, "Stewart, God has just told me you are going to write a book."

I replied, "Thanks for sharing that, but I don't really know if I am going to write a book."

In September 2015, my wife, Merilyn, and I took a couple of friends to lunch at Hillarys Boat Harbour, Perth, and during our conversation, one of them, Magdalena, said, "So Stewart, when are you going to write your book?"

"Why did you say that? I mean what made you say that?" I replied. "Thanks for sharing, but I don't really know if I am going to write a book."

"I have known since January," she said.

The word of God states in 2 Corinthians 13:1b (NKJV):

"By the mouth of two or three witnesses every word shall be established."

I still struggled because I knew that this book, if written, was going to challenge a sacred cow of teaching with the Pentecostal Christians, especially my dear pastor friends.

In October of 2015, I asked Magdalena's husband, who was the dean of a Bible college, if he would pray, as I needed confirmation on the writing of this book. One week later, he said, "The Holy Spirit told me, 'Stewart hears from Me,' and that you are to write the book." At last I had my third witness, as I had been asking God for three confirmations.

I ask you to be like the Bereans in the New Testament, who checked out everything to make sure it was correct. After you have read the book, please pray to God in the name of Jesus and ask the Holy Spirit what to do with your finances.

This book is not meant to be some sort of justification for a Christian failing to give to God's work. Christians under the New Covenant should give freely, as God loves a cheerful giver. 2 Corinthians 8:12–14 says that giving should not be a burden; we should be motivated to bring equality so that no one would be lacking or in need.

Matthew 10:8 says, "Give from the heart gladly."

2 Corinthians 9:7 says, "Be generous from a willing mind."

I encourage my Christian readers not to skip the section on the global financial system, as it is important to know how and why the financial Armageddon is coming.

I believe, when we dig beneath the surface and reveal the naked truth, that Christian blessings are based on grace. One of the greatest Bible teachers of the twentieth century, the late Derek Prince, stated, "The covenant of grace does not operate through laws enforced from without but through laws written by the Holy Spirit in the hearts of believers." When the Holy Spirit moves on the hearts of His people, He will make them like Himself: generous givers.

The main purpose for writing this book is because I want you to be set free from legalism, to have your joy return, and to live a prosperous life in Christ Jesus. Amen.

Disclaimer – Check with your doctor before starting an exercise program.

PART 1

Old Testament, Old Covenant

This might surprise a lot of Christians, but there were actually three distinct tithes under the Old Covenant.

In Numbers 18:24, there was a tithe to the Levites.

In Malachi 3:10–11, under the law of Moses, there was a tithe for the poor. This was based on Deuteronomy 14:28–29 (NKJV):

> At the end of every third year you shall bring out the tithe of your produce of that year, and store it up within your gates.
>
> And the Levite, because he has no portion nor inheritance with you, and the stranger, and the fatherless, and the widow who are within your gates, may come, and eat and be satisfied, that the LORD your God may bless you in all the work of your hand which you do.

And in Deuteronomy 14:22–23, 26 (NKJV), there was a festival tithe:

> You shall truly tithe all the increase of your grain that the field produces year by year.

> And you shall eat before the LORD your God, in the place where He chooses to make His name abide, the tithe of your grain and your new wine and your oil, of the firstborn of your herds and your flocks, that you may learn to fear the LORD your God always …

> And you shall spend that money for whatever your heart desires: for oxen or sheep, for wine or similar drink, for whatever your heart desires; you shall eat there before the LORD your God, and you shall rejoice, you and your household.

In Malachi 3:10 the tithe was only required to be paid every three years, so 10 percent divided by three is approximately 3 percent per annum. Now when you add the other two tithes (10 percent Festival tithe (Deut. 14:12, 22, 23, 26) + 10 percent Levite tithe (Num. 18:23) to the 3 percent, it equals 23 percent per annum.

We will see in greater detail that none of these applied to New Covenant Christians. We will also find that firstfruits in the New Testament/New Covenant of grace was Christ Himself and the believers in the first century.

Those who teach tithing fail to reveal that there were at least three mandatory food tithes required by the law of Moses. They also fail to reveal that there were many individuals in ancient Israel who did not earn their living by producing food and therefore did not tithe at all because it was not commanded of them. They only teach a spiritualised version of the one food tithe in Malachi 3:10, used to support the Old Testament Levitical ministry.

Ministers of the gospel are not Levitical ministry. They are not commanded to receive tithes. Unlike the Levitical ministry, they might work at other occupations to support themselves and often did in the New Testament. Nowadays, some do support themselves, but some don't.

The church plays on the fear that if you don't tithe, you will be cursed. The amazing truth is if you put Christians back under the Law, you rob them of New Covenant blessings. Christ's poverty at the cross was real, so why wouldn't the riches be real? What are the riches in Christ and riches in heavenly places? They are riches in forgiveness, wisdom, knowledge, grace, and fellowship with God.

The three scripture references below are the foundation for all New Testament believers:

> For if there is first a willing mind, it is accepted according to what one has, and not according to what he does not have.

For I do not mean that others should be eased, and you burdened:

> but by an equality, that now at this time your abundance may supply their lack, that their abundance also may supply your lack—that there may be an equality. (2 Corinthians 8:12–14 NKJV)

> For you know the grace of our Lord Jesus Christ, that though He was rich, yet for your sakes He became poor, that you through His poverty might become rich. (2 Corinthians 8:9 NKJV)

> For the law was given through Moses, but grace and truth came through Jesus Christ.

> (John 1:17 NKJV)

Christ's only statement about tithing validates the tithing of food for Jews living under the law of Moses. It does not validate believers continually tithing money. Christ and the church are the prophetic fulfilment of giving firstfruits in the Old Testament. Christ Himself and the church are the firstfruits.

When the Jerusalem Council in Acts 15 decided what aspects of the law of Moses that Gentile believers must keep, they did not validate tithing as a special exception. The Jerusalem Council did not set tithing money apart as a universal principle.

The practice of tithing actually comes from the seriously compromised Council of Tours in AD 567. The tithing of food was transformed into the tithing of money. This is a serious distortion of what the New Testament reveals. Jesus said in Matthew 15:9 that it was vain to worship Him from doctrines that they had invented.

Tithing money is incredibly unfair. It is extremely hard on the poor and very easy on the rich. There are numerous believers who have tithed for many years and are in serious debt. Some have seen their debts increase since they started tithing. And some believers who have renounced tithing as a legalistic practise and have given freely and generously as led by the Holy Spirit have seen blessings in their finances.

Laws in the form of obligations and requirements always stir up sin. Grace, on the other hand, gives believers the ability to give freely by faith.

> Then Jacob made a vow, saying, "If God will be with me, and will keep me in this way that I am going, and give me bread to eat, and clothing to put on,
>
> so that I come back to my father's house in peace; then the LORD shall be my God.
>
> And this stone, which I have set as a pillar, shall be God's house and of all that You give me I will surely give a tenth to You." (Genesis 28:20–22 NKJV)

First, the tithe was completely voluntary on Jacob's part.

Second, God must bless first.

Third, it was a once-only act.

And fourth, there was no evidence that Jacob taught his sons and daughters to tithe money.

Genesis 14:18–20 shows this was a voluntary tithe: a one-time act and not an entire income.

Hebrews 7:11–12 shows that the imperfect Old Covenant, with all of its legalistic law going through imperfect priests, has been abolished and replaced by a perfect and better New Covenant, with Christ as the perfect High Priest.

No writers in the New Testament stated we should tithe to Christ or anyone else. In Matthew 23:23, Jesus is speaking to the Jews under the Old Covenant before the cross and states that the food tithe should be kept. Now under the New Covenant, Christians are led by the Holy Spirit and give voluntarily from their heart.

Note: Mint, dill, and cumin are food spices referred to when speaking to the scribes and Pharisees, who were religious leaders under the law; whereas the disciples who are under the New Covenant, are not under the law but under grace, as shown in the following verses.

> So let each one give as he purposes in his heart, not grudgingly or of necessity; for God loves a cheerful giver.

> And God is able to make all grace abound toward you, that you always having all sufficiency in all things, may have an abundance for every good work. (2 Corinthians 9:7–8 NKJV)

Grace is not only the favour you don't deserve but also divine empowerment to succeed.

Please note in regards to giving that if you have not heard from the Holy Spirit, simply give what is in your heart. Remember: humanity looks on the outside but God looks on the inside. Entering God's system of finances requires faith in Christ, which releases abundant resources and the inner quality of peace. Whatever the Holy Spirit tells you to do, do it.

Now there is a very sobering scripture in Matthew 23:14 regarding the religious leaders. They were transforming a food tithe into a money tithe and telling these poor widows who were in abject poverty to give 10 percent of their income. This was the tipping point. They couldn't make their home payments, so many lost their homes.

It has been noted that this was not practiced in the early Christian church but gradually became common in the Roman Catholic Church in Western Europe by the sixth century. The Council of Tours in 567 and the Council of Macon in 585 advocated tithing. And it was made obligatory by civil law in the Carolingian Empire in 765 in England. The Reformation did not abolish tithing, and the practice was continued in the Roman Catholic Church and in Protestant countries, until it was gradually replaced by other forms of taxation. The Roman Catholic Church still prescribes tithes in countries where they are sanctioned by law, and some Protestant bodies consider tithes obligatory.

An encyclopaedia also comments that the Eastern Orthodox churches never accepted the idea of tithes, and Orthodox church members have never paid them.

There is a teaching that because Abraham tithed before the law of Moses, it should be okay to tithe in the New Covenant. Let's have a closer look at Matthew 23:23. In it, Jesus is talking to religious leaders who are still obeying the Old Covenant. Obviously, Jesus has not yet gone to the cross, and the New Covenant has not started.

Secondly, Abraham's one-time act of tithing does not validate the teaching of a lifetime of ongoing weekly tithing. It was also on the goods captured from war, which was far less than 10 percent of his entire income in the one-time act.

For twenty-one hundred years (from 4000 BC to 1900 BC) tithing was never mentioned. It's strange that God left out such a universal principle that modern-day preachers espouse today. Jesus, like you, can't mix oil and water in the natural. And you can't mix two entirely different covenants in two different dispensations.

Note: In four thousand years of biblical history, there are only two one-time acts of tithing money. Only those who got their income from the land were required to tithe.

The Gentiles did not know about tithing food, yet the council did not bring it to their attention. They clearly saw tithing as part of the law, just as circumcision was a part of the law.

Galatians 3:10 shows that we cannot cherry-pick parts of the law, including tithing. Adhering to any aspect of the law means we must observe it all. We cannot serve the law and a living saviour:

"For as many as are led by the Spirit of God, they are sons of God" (Romans 8:14 NKJV).

We as children of God in the New Covenant go from compulsory to voluntary, from law to relationship with Christ. There is freedom to live as a steward and to obey the Holy Spirit in all matters, including giving. At times, this may mean giving more than 10 percent, in obedience to the Lord.

After Merilyn and I sold our investment in gold, the $1,000 we gave to a person in need was 14.4 percent of the profit; we both purposed in our hearts to gladly give that amount. Paul the apostle, under the teaching of the Holy Spirit, wrote to the church at Corinth the way New Testament believers (many Jewish Christians) were to give cheerfully (2 Corinthians 9:7).

Paul, who wrote two-thirds of the New Testament, never said we were to give a definite percentage of our income. If tithing was meant to be a universal requirement of the New Testament/New Covenant, surely he would have mentioned it.

The Old and New Covenant Financial System

The confusion between these two systems is a major reason why many Christians do not prosper financially. What is the answer for New Covenant believers? We have already looked at Galatians 3:10, so with that in mind, now look at Galatians 3:13 (KJV): "Christ has redeemed us from the curse of the law, having become a curse for us, for it is written, 'Cursed is everyone who hangs on a tree.'"

Under the foundation of Old Covenant finances, God was going to give Abraham land, as seen in Genesis 12:6–7.

Eleven tribes received land, except the tribe of Levi. Now, every fiftieth year was the year of Jubilee, and back then, all debts were cancelled. Do Christian leaders mention all debts are going to be cancelled every fiftieth year? No, because we are no longer under the law of Moses. The three tithes are no longer applicable in the New Covenant. We can no longer cherry-pick parts of the law and spiritualise Malachi 3:10 ("Bring all the tithes into the storehouse, that there may be meat in my house, and prove me now herewith, says the LORD of hosts, if I will not open you the windows of heaven, and pour you out a blessing, that there shall not be room enough to receive it."). This was an offering that was taken up throughout the towns of Israel for the poor every three years.

Note: The system no longer exists in Israel and has never existed in Gentile nations.

Deuteronomy 15:1 shows that under the Old Covenant, debts were cancelled every seven years, but in the New Testament, Christians do not have their debts cancelled, ever. We need to examine the three different tithes in the Old Testament more closely.

The first tithe was to support the Levites who were the only tribe that was not given land to make a living. Almighty God saw to it that the other eleven tribes supported them with 10 percent of food (not money) called the "tithe."

History showed in Numbers 18:24 that this system ultimately failed and was the harbinger to a better covenant.

The first tithe was the firstfruits of the harvest and the firstfruits of the food animals, meaning the firstborn of the flock and herds.

"Firstfruits" is used in the New Testament to describe Christ Himself and the believers in the first century. Christ Himself is the firstfruits, and the first-century church was the firstfruits to God. The tithe was only on things that God alone grew and not what man created by his own labours or skills (Leviticus 27:30).

Note: Christian leaders today can own businesses and property and work a job for a living, as did Paul, who was a tent maker in the New Testament.

A very important point not mentioned by most ministers was about the produce of food. Tithing amongst the children of Israel was connected only to Canaan; the land that God gave to them. In AD 125, the Romans renamed it Palestenias, which is now called Palestine.

"Speak to the children of Israel, and say to them: 'When you come into the land which I give to you, and reap its harvest, then you shall bring a sheaf of the firstfruits of your harvest to the priest" (Leviticus 23:10 NKJV).

Let's take a look at what happened in Exodus 36:5–6, when the people of Israel gave freely from the heart. They gave so much that they were asked to stop. When God's people are not being coerced by legal requirements, they are able to display very gracious giving.

The second tithe was for the poor, the widow, the orphan, and the foreigner. This food tithe was stored locally to support those in need. In Deuteronomy 14:28–29, the poor did not tithe at all; they had no harvest to provide the tithe. This is not mentioned by our ministers. Tithing money today is incredibly hard on the poor and easy on the rich. Teaching the poor to tithe their income is a heavy burden that Christ never intended them to carry.

Malachi chapter 3 mentions the poor tithe; it is a very popular text used in the church today to teach the tithing of money. This passage is often wrongly taught as pertaining to the Levites and priests and then spiritualised to apply to the ministry of the church.

"Bring all the tithes into the storehouse, that there may be food in My house, and try Me now in this," says the LORD of hosts, "If I will not open for you the windows of heaven, and pour out for you such blessing that there will not be room enough to receive it" (Malachi 3:10 NKJV).

The church has often sincerely but ignorantly misused this passage by spiritualising it. The storehouse becomes the local church, rather than the literal Jewish town's storehouse for the poor. The literal food becomes money. The windows of heaven is some sort of supernatural blessing, but is actually the literal sky that is used in Genesis to describe the flood that caused the rain.

Unfortunately, the money collected by misusing this passage is not generally used to support the poor. Some churches do have a food ministry, but only a fraction of the money goes to the poor; too often, money is spent on supporting the church ministry and on improving the building.

The New Testament way is based on 2 Corinthians 9:7, 8:12–14, and 8:9.

Please note that the rule for understanding the Bible is to take it literally, even where it is clearly figurative or supernatural.

I have been in Pentecostal churches for forty-six years and also attended Bible college for three years, so I can attest to the teachings of pastors who spiritualised Malachi 3:10–11 to bring (as an act of worship) the full amount of your tithe (10 percent of your ongoing income) into the storehouse (local church) so that there may be food (spiritual food) in my house (the local church) and prove me.

Put me to the test, give Me an opportunity to prove Myself and you will see that I will open the windows of heaven to you … and pour out on you so much (financial material) blessing that you will not have room enough to contain it. Then I will rebuke protect your income from the devourer, the devil, for you—I will stop the thief (the devil) from destroying the fruit (money, material goods) of your labours.

Now here is the true literal meaning of Malachi 3:10–11:1: Bring the full amount of (the once every three years) food tithe into My storehouse (the local storehouse for the poor and needy), that there may be food (real food) in My storehouse and prove Me now (during the time of the law of Moses) by it, and you will see that I will open the windows of heaven (the sky) to you (Jews growing crops)—and pour out so much blessing (rain) that you will not have room enough to contain it (the harvest) Then I will rebuke the devourer (those things that destroy crops: insects, bad weather) who may not destroy the fruits of the ground (the crops) nor will your vine in the field cast (drop prematurely) its grapes.

Note: this Old Testament prophet was living under the law of Moses. The apostles and writers of the New Testament did not see this prophecy as applying to the church at all.

The third tithe is the festival tithe. This tithe was actually for the benefit of the consumer. 10 percent of the harvest of grain, new wine, and olive oil was to be saved and splurged in a great party in Jerusalem. This party was three times a year. Can you imagine your minister encouraging you to put away 10 percent of your pay to have three large parties a year with a large group of your friends at an exotic location?

The Festival Tithe

Each Israelite was commanded to go to Jerusalem three times a year to celebrate these festivals, under the law of Moses.

This is the commandment of the festival tithe (Deuteronomy 14: 22–23 NLT): "You must set aside a tithe of your crops – one-tenth of all crops you harvest each year. Bring this tithe to the designated place of worship – the place the LORD your God chooses for his name to be honoured – and eat it there in his presence. This applies to your tithes of grain, new wine, olive oil, and the firstborn males of your flocks and herds. Doing this will always teach you to fear the LORD your God."

It was strictly agricultural and husbandry. This festival tithe could be sold for money if the distance to bring the harvest and animals was too great (Deuteronomy 14:24–26).

In Leviticus 27:30–31 (NLT), God so discouraged any part of the food tithe to be connected to money that a 20 percent penalty would be imposed:

"One-tenth of the produce of the land, whether grain from the fields or fruit from the trees, belongs to the LORD and must be set apart to him as holy.

If you want to buy back the LORD's tenth of the grain or fruit, you must pay its value, plus 20 percent."

So 10% + 1/5th of the 10% = 12% of the value of food, if he wanted to bring money instead of food. Since you cannot cherry-pick, that is, pay only one of the three tithes, if the three tithes were paid properly, it would average 23 percent of the farming produce or livestock. Why 23 percent? Because the tithe (10 percent) for the poor and needy was presented to the local storehouse every three years, approximately 3 percent. So 10% + 10% + 3% = 23%.

God was commanding that percentage, in acknowledgement of the fact that only He can produce food. There was no tithing on what man produced by his personal labour, skill, or knowledge; that is why the tithe was called "holy."

Note: Sometimes, coins were used in offerings, but not in tithing.

This will come as a surprise to some Christian leaders: God did not require a tithe (10 percent) of food or money from other kinds of occupations. There were lawyers, scribes, merchants, weavers, innkeepers, and tent makers who did not pay a tithe since they were not producing food. Paul the apostle, a tent maker, in all his New Testament writings, never mentioned that Christians were to tithe.

The Jews who lived outside Canaan (renamed Palestine by the Romans in 125), who farmed or raised flocks, did not have a commandment to tithe. The mandatory system of financing commanded by God was part of Israel's taxation system. This was designed to support Levites and priests who among other religious and civic duties were judges, teachers, police, and medical authorities.

Note: The Israelites were paying the food tithe the same way we pay taxes; not to do so was a serious violation of the law of Moses.

Some have said Israel was a simple agrarian culture, where crops were their income. Israel did use copper, silver, and gold coins; in fact, it had a sophisticated system of finance, loans, investments, promissory notes, interest, and collateral.

The Lord Jesus before He went to the cross was speaking to Jews who were producing food under the law of Moses. He tells us tithing involves food, not money, and that tithing is not a universal principle; it is not the weighty matter of the law.

New Testament Giving

Saul, who had an encounter with the risen Christ on the road to Damascus, and later was known as the Apostle Paul, has been attributed by scholars to have written two-thirds of the New Testament, and not once did he tell his Jewish and Gentile converts to tithe to the local church. The early church did not teach tithing.

In the book of Acts chapter 15, at the first apostolic council at Jerusalem, the leaders met to determine what aspects of the law of Moses that Gentile (non-Jewish) believers should keep:

"For it seemed good to the Holy Spirit, and to us, to lay upon you no greater burden than these necessary things: that you abstain from things offered to idols, from blood, from things strangled, and from sexual immorality. If you keep yourselves from these, you will do well. Farewell" (Acts 15:28–29 NKJV).

The apostolic council did not believe that Gentiles had to keep any aspect of the law.

Note: The (New Testament) Apostle Paul encouraged believers to save weekly for a one-time gift to help the poor believers in Jerusalem. This in no way resembles the mandatory 10 percent of your gross income to be paid every week, as taught by the Pentecostal churches of today.

"Now concerning the collection for the saints, as I have given orders to the churches of Galatia, so you must do also:

On the first day of the week let each one of you lay something aside, storing up as he may prosper, that there be no collections when I come" (1 Corinthians 16: 1–2 NKJV).

Note: The Council of Christian leaders, apostles, and others did not embrace circumcision or tithing money as a special universal principle for anyone to practise.

Tithing money was a later invention of the Medieval Roman Catholic Church. A forgiven child of God is completely free from debt to God. The New Covenant of grace has wiped out indebtedness to God, paid in full by our Lord Jesus Christ. The money tithe, which is really an ongoing temple tax, violates the principle that ministry is an expression of grace. Paul does not state a percentage as a standard; the standard for giving is what we purpose in our heart.

Tithing is commendable, but the Bible does not command it for New Testament believers. Ten percent is too little for some and is impossible for others. New Covenant believers give from the heart because they want to see people come into God's Kingdom, not because it is traditionally based on an Old Covenant in another dispensation.

Out of the 980 million people who go to bed hungry, some have become Christians and cannot afford to give 10 percent of their meagre income. Those of us who have some discretionary income, who love Christ, should gladly help the poor. The Lord promises if you give to the poor, you lend to the Lord, and He will repay.

Would giving dent your lifestyle, or do you make lifestyle choices first, with giving as an afterthought? If you are wealthy, perhaps you could re-examine your stewardship decisions; maybe you could adjust your lifestyle. Do you really need more than one car or a number of sports coats? How many pairs of shoes do you need? How much use do you get out of a luxury boat or a holiday house? Being wealthy does not prove tithing is the answer; there are many wealthy unbelievers who have given nothing into the church or to charities.

From time to time, it should cost you something. The Old Testament tells the story of King David, who tried to buy a threshing floor from Araunah to erect an altar to the Lord (2 Samuel 24:18–25). The key verse is "Nor will I offer burnt offerings to the LORD my God with that which costs me nothing."

King David obeyed God and humbly went to Araunah; he politely explained that he needed his threshing floor and why he needed it. Araunah gladly gave it, but King David would not take advantage of him and insisted that he should pay for it. There was a good heart and an attitude of obedience and generosity between the two men, and the plague was withdrawn from Israel.

Think sacrifice instead of tithe. This may require a paradigm shift in your thinking and take some getting used to, but it is the best way to answer the difficult question of how much should I give? We should not take things from another person like it is our right to have it; we should always keep an attitude of putting others first and have respect for them and their property.

Paul the apostle wrote the answer in 2 Corinthians 8:12–14 (KJV):

"For if there be first a willing mind, it is accepted according to what one has, and not according to what he does not have.

For I do not mean that others should be eased, and you burdened; but by an equality, that now at this time your abundance may supply their lack, that their abundance also may supply your lack - that there may be equality."

Remember: Anything that is made compulsory is a tax. People are under income taxes, excise taxes, state taxes, and so on. Giving from the heart is the New Covenant way to build the kingdom of God on this earth.

The New Covenant produces children of God. The best the Old Covenant could do was to produce servants for God, as they were not yet born again. They were born again when Jesus went down to paradise and preached to them:

"And when he had come into the house, Jesus anticipated him, saying, 'What do you think, Simon? From whom do the kings of the earth take customs or taxes, from their sons or from strangers?'

Peter said to Him, 'From strangers.'" Jesus said to him, 'Then the sons are free'" (Matthew 17:25–26 NKJV).

The key point is, Christ says that the New Covenant children of God are free from the financial requirements and commandments of the Old Covenant law of Moses.

Matthew 14:19–21 is Christ's way of visually teaching the disciples (and us) that others can be served first, and there will be plenty left over to take care of ourselves and our families. The five loaves and two fish were multiplied to feed everyone present, plus twelve baskets were left over. This shows how amazing is the provision of our God.

John 1:17 (NKJV) says, "For the law was given through Moses, *but* grace and truth came through Jesus Christ."

In the New Covenant, Christ has fulfilled all God's requirements, and now we receive grace and mercy as a result of believing in Christ and His work at Calvary. Believers heal the sick and have financial miracles on the basis of Christ's righteousness, not their own righteousness.

In 1 Timothy 6:18–19, Paul tells Timothy to instruct the people to do good, to be rich in good works, and to be generous and ready to share. But in Jude 1:11–12, unfortunately, there are some Christian leaders who care only for themselves; they serve for pay and not out of love for Christ and the people of God.

Our heavenly Father does not forget the birds of the air, and therefore He cannot forget us. So, what is the New Testament standard for giving? The standard is what we purpose in our hearts. You cannot buy God's favour. But you must have a generous heart and be willing to give to a brother who is in need.

God owns all things, both physical and spiritual. He owns the air that we breathe and every breath that we take. We have temporary possession and control of these things, and we owe nothing to God but praise, worship, and gratitude. Why? Because Christ paid for our indebtedness at Calvary. The world's financial system produces anxiety and greed and too often a selfish attitude. God's financial system is higher than the world's financial system, built on hidden abundance. Most of God's resources are hidden in Christ, but they are available to all who wish to walk as Christ's servants.

Entering into God's system of finances requires faith in Christ, which releases abundant resources and the inner quality of peace. God rewards obedience; just do whatever God tells you to do, and you will be blessed, along with the person you are assisting. Faithful and tested stewards will see ongoing supernatural increase and unusual supernatural intervention by Christ in their finances.

The Meaning of "Deity"

"*Dei*" is "steward" in the Greek.

Oikonomos: literally, "the one who arranges the house."

"*Ity*" means "we are the children of God and the servants of Christ."

"And the Lord said, "Who then is that faithful and wise steward, whom his master will make ruler over his household, to give them their portion of food in due season?

Blessed is that servant whom his master will find so doing when he comes" (Luke 12:42–43 NKJV).

A steward is a servant. On returning, the master (Jesus) will promote a faithful steward with more resources and people to care for.

Paul did not own the mysteries of God. He was a steward of them (1 Corinthians 4:1–2).

All our financial resources and physical property are a stewardship from God. All our gifts, ministries, and vocations, spiritual and vocational, are a stewardship from God.

We must love Christ supremely and passionately above all other things. We must put aside all that competes with our love for Christ. God always rewards obedience and a passion for Him. We must wait on the Holy Spirit, and learn to hear His voice, so we only obey His voice.

In Matthew 19:16–17 Christ reveals you cannot own or possess eternal life since it belongs to God. You can only enter into eternal life by relationship with God. Human wisdom and effort cannot convince a rich man or woman to become Christ's steward. It must be a work of the Holy Spirit. The rich young ruler was working for the reward of keeping the commandments. Christ was calling him to a higher level, requiring relationship, radical trust and faith in God for the outcome.

"Stewardship" means one who arranges the house. The master (Christ) puts a steward in charge of His people and His resources.

We are expected by God to use that which we have been given, faithfully and sensibly, to serve Christ as we serve others. Our financial resources and physical property are a stewardship from God. Christ always rewards fruitfulness with additional resources. The divine use of money is not security but is relational. Money should be used to build the kingdom, church, and family friendships. This would include evangelism of the lost as well as developing existing relationships with other believers.

In Colossians 2:2–3, Christ Himself is the hidden treasure that every believer should seek.

Matthew 6:21 (NKJV) says, "For where your treasure is, there your heart will be also."

The word "heart" incorporates the entire mental, emotional, moral, and spiritual elements of a person.

The word "Lord" in the Greek is *Kurios*, which means one who rules or exercises power.

The Father cares for us not because we do something, but because we are something. We are His beloved children, redeemed by the precious blood of Jesus.

The word "kingdom" in the Greek is *basileia*, which means sphere of God's rule over us on earth.

The word "righteousness" in the Greek is *diakaiosene*, which means actions towards humanity.

The forgiveness of our debt of sin will be revoked if we fail to forgive others (Matthew 18:23–29).

"And you being dead in your trespasses and the uncircumcision of your flesh, He has made alive together with Him, having forgiven you all trespasses,

having wiped out the handwriting of requirements that was against us, which was contrary to us. And He has taken it out of the way, having nailed it to the cross" (Colossians 2:13–14 NKJV).

The certificate of debt has been cancelled. We are led by the Spirit of Christ from obligation to love, from legalism to grace, from bondage to freedom, and from slavery to sonship.

Sacred Cows

Jesus said to the religious Pharisees, "Your tradition has made the word of God of no effect." It may surprise you that tradition can nullify the word of God. We are now going to kill some sacred cows that have kept tens of thousands of Christians in bondage to the law and have kept them from experiencing the wonderful joy and peace and freedom that has been purchased by our Lord Jesus Christ.

Sacred Cow No. 1: The Tithe Is the Lord's

This statement implies that the tithe automatically carries over to the New Covenant, even after Jesus fulfilled all the requirements of the law when He went to the cross and said, "It is finished." Redemption, sickness, and poverty now are subject to a new enforcement: the power of the Holy Spirit, which every man, woman, and child could have.

The statement is based on Leviticus 27:30 (NKJV):

"And all the tithe of the land, whether of the seed of the land or of the fruit of the tree, is the LORD's. It is holy to the LORD."

The Lord is speaking to Moses and giving him instructions to give to the children of Israel. Please note: These instructions are not given to the body of Christ. There is no tithe in the New Covenant, so they cannot apply to us.

"Therefore, if anyone is in Christ, he is a new creation; old things have passed away; behold, all things have become new" (2 Corinthians 5:17 NKJV).

We are to be led by the Holy Spirit, not by carnal principles like tithing, which were necessary for men who were not born again.

Note: Most of the erroneous teaching on tithing comes from one thing: People are trying to mix Old Covenant principles with a life in Christ, like oil and water, they don't mix.

Sacred Cow No. 2: If You Don't Tithe, You Are a God Robber

Under the Old Covenant in Malachi 3:8, the tithe was the Lord's, and the children of Israel were robbing God when they didn't give to Him. We have a new and better covenant through our spiritual union with Christ, and we share His relationship with the Father. We have gone from rules and formulas to a relationship with Christ.

We really are stewards of everything God has given us; everything really belongs to Him. The issue is not tithing; it is following the Holy Spirit's leading at all times. How do we prosper? The next thing He (the Holy Spirit) tells you to do, do it. We all love to give our children good gifts, and so does God. He loves His children and gives them good gifts.

We no longer live on the level of tithing; we live on a higher calling of absolute abandonment to God and His purposes on earth. Our standard today is not 10 percent; it is Christ Himself, who gave everything.

Sacred Cow No. 3: A Curse Will Come on You if You Don't Tithe

God gave Israel the law over one thousand years before the Prophet Malachi spoke those words in Malachi 3:9. God told Israel very clearly what the blessing would be for keeping the law and what the curse would be for breaking it. There is no curse upon us in Christ; it is not part of our Covenant.

"Christ has redeemed us from the curse of the law, having become a curse for us (for it is written, 'Cursed is everyone who hangs on a tree')" (Galatians 3:13 NKJV).

Note: If you put yourself back under any part of the law, you will put yourself back under the whole law (Galatians 3:10).

Sacred Cow No. 4: We Are Commanded to Prove God with the Tithe

Just as there was a curse for breaking the law, there was a blessing for keeping the law. Israel was challenged to keep the law of tithing and thereby put God to the test. Malachi 3:10 was not written to the church.

The New Testament/New Covenant is not works based, and we are not cursed for not giving financially. The New Covenant does not work by general standards like the tithe. It is administered by the Holy Spirit in a way that is unique to each person and situation:

"For as many as are led by the Spirit of God, these are sons of God" (Romans 8:14 NKJV).

Faith is what God is looking for. He does not need your money; where He is living, the streets are paved with gold. We need to have compassion for people around us who are in need and to look out for each other.

"But without faith it is impossible to please Him, for he who comes to God must believe that He is, and that He is rewarder of those who diligently seek Him" (Hebrews 11:6 NKJV).

As soon as you add your works to grace, then it is not grace. Grace is God's part, and faith is our part. How does faith come? By hearing the word of God (Romans 10:17) and praying in the Holy Spirit (Jude 1: 20).

Under the law, God had servants, and if they kept the law, He would bless them. God has sons (that includes women, just as the Bride of Christ includes men), and as sons, we have a relationship with our heavenly Father, the Lord Jesus Christ. The unconverted Jews tried to put the Jews who had become Christians back under the law. The Old Testament Jews said they could have Christ plus some parts of the law of Moses. Christians simply have a different way of life than the Old Testament saints. The book of Galatians is a book of freedom for the New Testament saints.

Note: If prosperity or any other covenant blessing depended on the tithe, then the tithe would be purchasing our heavenly blessing, not the blood of Jesus.

The New Covenant is a blood covenant, not a tithe covenant, when it comes to prosperity. In the Old Covenant, the shed blood was the covering of sin. The tithe was part of the provision blessing. In the new grace-based covenant, the foundation is 2 Corinthians 8:9.

Faith draws the blessing from the Father, not the tithe.

Sacred Cow No. 5: Jesus Taught Tithing

In Matthew 23:23, Jesus is talking to religious leaders, not His disciples. The religious leaders were still under the law. Jesus obviously hasn't gone to the cross, and the New Covenant wasn't ratified until blood was poured out, Jesus's blood.

Jews merely confirmed that the people Jesus was speaking of were under the law and that tithing was part of their covenant obligation.

"The law and the prophets were until John. Since that time the kingdom of God has been preached, and everyone is pressing into it" (Luke 16:16 NKJV).

Here, we see a change of covenants was about to take place. Jesus, walking through the dusty streets of Galilee, was demonstrating what this New Covenant was going to look like:

"Most assuredly, I say to you, he who believes in Me, the works that I do he will do also; and greater works than these he will do, because I go to My Father" (John 14:12 NKJV).

Note: God has put His own nature in the born-again Christian. When the church finds the revelation of their union with Christ, they will give from such a loving heart attitude that they will have to be told to stop giving, instead of constantly being harangued to start giving.

Sacred Cow No. 6: Tithing Qualifies You to Receive More from God

The Holy Spirit knows what is best to give in every situation. He knows all about you and your situation and how to take you to the next level of trust. It is exciting to abandon to God and develop a relationship of trust in your giving to God. Legalistic tithing is not relational.

The goal of stewardship is to use all resources wisely, by the infinite wisdom and knowledge of the Holy Spirit

Note: A steward is responsible for another person's wealth.

Sacred Cow No. 7: "Honour the Lord with Your Substance and with the Firstfruits of All Your Increase" Means to Tithe

Honouring the Lord with your firstfruits in Proverbs 3:9–10 has nothing to do with tithing.

Solomon was speaking to the people of his day, who were living under the law. Firstfruits was a distinctly different offering than the tithe; it was voluntary and had no set amount for its size. In the New Covenant, we can expect the blessings of God to be upon us as we abide in Christ and live for Him by faith, as Paul said in 2 Corinthians 9:6–8:

"But this I say; He who sows sparingly will also reap sparingly, and he who sows bountifully will also reap bountifully.

So let each one give as he purposes in his heart, not grudgingly or of necessity; for God loves a cheerful giver.

And God is able to make all grace abound toward you, that you, always having all sufficiency in all things, may have an abundance for every good work."

Sacred Cow No. 8: Tithing Puts God First in Your Life

Many people tithe because they sincerely believe if they don't, a curse will come upon them, and if they do, they will be blessed. But Christ has redeemed us from the curse of the law (Galatians 3:13).

They may tithe faithfully, but God is not first in their heart.

Note: People who are trying to put God first in their lives by tithing do not have a revelation of life in Christ in the New Covenant. The good news: when they do get the revelation, their giving will be Spirit led and a true expression of the love of God in their heart.

Sacred Cow No. 9: If Everyone Tithed, Churches Would Have Plenty of Money

Yes, the churches would have more money if everyone tithed, but tithing is not God's solution to a teaching which is contrary to grace or truth.

Note: If the true message of the New Covenant of life in union with Christ was preached, we would see the Holy Spirit work in the people's hearts, and church attendance would increase. There would be enough financial giving to do anything the Lord directs.

In the 1906 Azuza Street Revival, it was announced that no offerings were going to be taken up. But the Holy Spirit led people to give, and they had all expenses met. This amazingly covered three services per day, seven days per week, for three years.

Merilyn and I told our home church, "We are not taking up money, we don't want your money," and they still bring us money and say that God told them to give it to us, and that they want to do it. The money goes on the books for our discipleship lessons and to the homeless people when we go on the street, evangelising on Fridays, and to the mission we support in India.

Note: If ministers would trust their members to give as the Holy Spirit led them, or as they purposed in their heart, they would have more than enough. Most ministers only pick one of the three tithes mentioned in the Old Testament and so are not even preaching the whole truth of the Old Testament. When people are Spirit led in their giving, there is a real blessing on their lives.

Sacred Cow No. 10: Heaven Will Be Shut up Against You if You Don't Tithe

Under the Old Covenant, man was governed by rules for blessings and curses; it was the carrot and the stick, an eye for an eye, and a tooth for a tooth. It was the best God could do with them, as they didn't have the Holy Spirit dwelling in them.

"Do you not know that your body is the temple of the Holy Spirit who is in you, whom you have from God, and you are not your own?" (1 Corinthians 6:19 NKJV).

If the people of Israel broke the law, Leviticus 26:1 (NKJV) says, "You shall not make idols for yourselves; neither a carved image nor a sacred pillar shall you rear up for yourselves; nor shall you set up an engraved stone in your land, to bow down to it."

God said He would make their Heaven as iron (no rain) and earth as brass. There would be a reduction in food production—in reality, a curse.

Note: Since tithing is not part of our covenant, failure to tithe is not the source of our problems, and it consequently is not the solution to our problems. Our problem is disobedience.

Sacred Cow No. 11: How Do We Get Our Needs Met if We Don't Tithe?

Christians have more faith in an Old Testament formula than they do in a God who has committed to be a father to them. They do not realise how well God is providing for millions of Christians who do not tithe. There are also millions of nonbelievers who are more prosperous than Christians, and they certainly don't tithe.

Sacred Cow No. 12: You Can't Be Blessed if You Only Give Offerings

This is what is implied by modern-day ministers. When the poor Christians were going through a famine in Jerusalem, Apostle Paul encouraged them to give. It was not a collection for full-time ministers. The result is 2 Corinthians 9:6 (NKJV):

"He who sows sparingly, will reap sparingly, and he who sows bountifully will also reap bountifully."

In the correct context, the blessing did not depend on the person being a tither. Paul never once mentioned a fixed percentage of income to be going to the early church. He said lay aside an amount according to how God has prospered you, and that was in the context of having to be able to give Paul some money so he could give to the poor Christians, not full-time ministers.

Legalistic Nature of Tithing

There are many different opinions from preachers on how tithing should be done. The Holy Spirit has one simple method: give as you purpose in your heart on all forms of income.

Here are some issues that arise when the congregation is put back under the Old Testament law of tithing:

- Do I tithe on the gross or the net pay?
- Do I tithe on my superannuation pay-out?
- Do I tithe on my pension?
- Do I tithe if my spouse doesn't agree to it?

- Do members tithe back to the church that pays them?
- Do I tithe on money given to me for a missionary trip?
- Do I tithe on child support payments?

Note: The fact that so many questions have to be asked shows that it is not an inward working of the Holy Spirit.

Many struggling Christian families are tithing, and although some churches look prosperous, the bread winners are living lives of economic desperation. It is not Christ that is motivating them; they are trying to fulfil a law that they have been given. New wine cannot be contained in old wine skins. Your new relationship with God, as a son through Jesus Christ, cannot be expressed through the former ways of living before the resurrection.

Life in Christ does not work by following the ways of men who were not born again. Sons of God live by the life and power of Christ, who is in them, not by a religious system of rewards and punishments that are designed to control their behaviour:

"That the righteous requirement of the law might be fulfilled in us who do not walk according to the flesh but according to the Spirit" (Romans 8:4 NKJV).

Note: Sons of God includes women, just like the Bride of Christ includes men; these are Christians who are empowered to prosper financially by the grace of God. As they follow the Holy Spirit and do the will of God, they will prosper.

We can all work as PHD Christians: We *Pray*, we *Heal* the sick, and we *Deliver* people from demonic oppression.

We are blessed to be a blessing. You can't help the poor if you are one yourself. God almighty through Jesus Christ has given us a route out of the poverty trap. Sons of God have the same relationship to the Father as did the Jewish people. Since tithing is not a part of the Jewish relationship now that Jesus has been resurrected, it is not a part of ours either.

"But when the fullness of the time had come, God sent forth His Son, born of a woman, born under the law,

to redeem those who were under the law, that we might receive the adoption as sons" (Galatians 4:4–5 NKJV).

Note: Tithing was a crude system of stewardship: one law for everyone, everywhere, at all times. The Holy Spirit was not working directly and uniquely within each person in every situation. If you must have a formula, then here it is: "Whatever the Holy Spirit tells you to do, do it."

PART 2

Grace: The New Covenant

Since we are going to hear this word "grace" a lot, I think it is important to understand its full meaning.

A poll was taken in the United States, asking, "What does 'grace' mean?" 98 percent gave the common meaning, and 2 percent said that it meant divine empowerment, to take you above your own natural ability to succeed. Grace is God's part, that is, favour you do not deserve and faith is our part.

In the New Testament, God has not established a specific law, like that of the Old Testament, requiring Christians to set aside for Him a tenth of their income. The covenant of grace does not operate through laws enforced from without but through laws written by the Holy Spirit in the hearts of believers (2 Corinthians 8:12–14 and 9:7). When the Holy Spirit moves on the hearts of His people, He will make them like Himself: generous givers.

"In that He says, "A new covenant," He has made the first obsolete. Now what is becoming obsolete and growing old is ready to vanish away" (Hebrews 8:13 NKJV).

Therefore, we do not live under two separate covenants; the old one is obsolete, and the new one is better (Hebrews 8:6). A liberal heart, full of gratitude, brings God's blessings.

New Covenant Grace

New Covenant Christians, empowered by the Holy Spirit, which now dwells in their human spirits, can live a life of freedom and not be in bondage. Here is a contrast between legalism and Christianity, or rules verses relationship:

The Way of Legalism	The Way of Grace
Fears people	Gives reverence to God
Shows contempt towards God	Regrets sin
Is a man pleaser	Is confident of God's love
Studies to gain approval, is puffed up and proud	Has Godly discernment and is humble
Is controlling	Shares responsibility
Applies the law to others	Is gracious towards others
Finds fault in others	Is understanding and compassionate
Is self-absorbed	Esteems others
Goes to church out of duty or tradition.	Loves attending church, enjoys fellowship
Cannot admit their faults	Apologises for any wrongdoing
Lives by a set of rules	Overflows with God's love from within
Is carnally motivated	Is Holy Spirit led
Is religiously traditional	Depends on the Holy Spirit
Does not prosper	Is fruitful and glorifies God

Legalism is a spiritual rut, seeking to gain acceptance from God and people on the basis of performance. Tithing pleases man, but giving from the heart as the Holy Spirit directs is liberating; it takes joy in a relationship with God that is very satisfying.

Note: We are saved by grace (Ephesians 2:8–9 NKJV): "For by grace you have been saved through faith, and that not of yourselves; it is the gift of God, not of works, lest anyone should boast." We are healed by grace (1 Peter 2:24 NKJV): "Who Himself bore our sins in His own body on the tree, that we, having died to sins, might live for righteousness - by whose stripes you were healed." And we prosper by grace (2 Corinthians 8:9 NKJV): "For you know the grace of our Lord Jesus Christ, that though He was rich, yet for your sakes He became poor, that you through His poverty might become rich."

The New Covenant is initiated and ratified when blood is shed. The death of Christ had to happen for the New Covenant to be valid and in force. Even the first covenant had to be ratified by blood:

"Therefore not even the first covenant was dedicated without blood.

For when Moses had spoken every precept to all the people according to the law, he took the blood of calves and goats, with water, scarlet wool and hyssop, and sprinkled both the book itself and all the people.

Saying, 'This is the blood of the Covenant which God has commanded you'" (Hebrews 9:18–20 NKJV).

The New Covenant has both similarities and differences with the Old Covenant of law. It is different because it is not based on obedience to law but on grace through faith in Jesus Christ. It is similar because a covenant is made with God. Jesus Christ, God in human flesh, had to die before we could have the New Covenant. Always remember: When Jesus was walking on the earth, he was speaking to people still living under the law, even though the actual words are in the New Testament, the words "It is finished" had not been uttered. All the requirements of the law had not been fulfilled until His blood had been shed.

The Bible shows that there is a transition to the New Covenant from the Old Covenant in Luke 16:16 (NKJV):

"The law and the prophets were until John. Since that time the kingdom of God has been preached, and everyone is pressing into it."

According to Jesus, the Old Covenant proclamation of law ended at John the Baptist's ministry. When Jesus spoke of faith or believing, it is strong proof that He was not preaching the law.

Apostle Paul said, "The law is not of faith" (Galatians 3:12 NKJV). Believing is a condition of the New Covenant.

Jesus was sent by the Father to preach the kingdom of God. He was not sent to preach the law. Faith is a very important subject to cover, and there are more than one hundred references to faith and believing in the gospel. The great number of times that Jesus Christ refers to faith or believing reveals that He is not preaching the law, rather He is preaching a strong New Covenant message.

Provision by God's Grace

Many years ago, a friend of mine was running a department where he worked and offered me a position. On the day that I resigned from my current job, my friend was fired; his boss was cutting costs and said they could manage without him. So I told my boss that I no longer had a job to go to, and he said that it was too bad I had shown my hand; they had just had a farewell party for me and given me a present, so I could go.

A few weeks prior, another friend told me there was a position vacant where he worked if I wanted it; luckily, when I phoned him to let him know that I didn't need it, I couldn't get through on the line. So here I was without a job, and I phoned this friend to see if the position was still available. It was, but I had to wait one week to start, and they paid fortnightly. We went three weeks without pay, and that last week, we had no money for food.

We were amazed as we watched our food be multiplied; it all ran out on the day that I had money to go food shopping. It is times like that when we can still feel God's love, grace, and mercy; it is very reassuring that Jesus really does hold us up in the palm of His right hand and will never let us fall.

Jesus says faith without works is dead (that is, faith without corresponding action is dead). God's word will go from your head to your heart if you spend time getting to know the Holy Spirit and His word.

In Luke 7:22, Christ says that He is preaching the gospel. He says nothing about the law and the prophets. The word "kingdom" appears 117 times in the gospels. The word "law" appears only thirty-one times. None of these references to the law suggest that Christ was operating under the law or preaching the law of Moses.

Paul describes his ministry to the elders at Ephesus:

"So that I may finish my race with joy, and the ministry which I received from the Lord Jesus, to testify to the gospel of the grace of God.

And indeed now I know that you all, among whom I have gone preaching the kingdom of God, will see my face no more" (Acts 20:24b–25 NKJV).

To say that the gospel of the kingdom of God is not about grace but about the law would be disagreeing with the Apostle Paul, who explained that it is found throughout the gospels to always be about grace and has never been about the law.

In Acts 28:23b, Paul explained via the law and the prophets that Christ was the fulfilment, the completion, of both the law of Moses and the prophets.

Galatians 3:12 (NKJV) says, "Yet the law is not faith, but the man who does them shall live by them." Since the law is not of faith, the strong emphasis on faith in the ministry of Jesus Christ in the gospels reveals He is not operating under the law, but by grace (Ephesians 2:8–9).

How does a person receive this New Covenant faith?

Romans 10:17 (NKJV) says, "So then faith comes by hearing, and hearing by the word of God."

And Jude 1: 20 (NKJV) says, "But you, beloved, building yourselves up on your most holy faith, praying in the Holy Spirit."

The Holy Spirit mentioned here is the supernatural language given to you by Jesus. It means you can now speak a perfect prayer language to God.

1 Corinthians 14:2 (NKJV) says, "For he who speaks in a tongue does not speak to men but to God, for no one understands him; however, in the spirit he speaks mysteries."

This wonderful truth is reinforced in Romans 8:26 (NKJV): "Likewise the Spirit also helps in our weaknesses. For we do not know what we should pray for as we ought, but the Spirit Himself makes intercession for us with groanings which cannot be uttered."

Note: When the Spirit has a capital "S," it refers to the Holy Spirit, and when the spirit has a lowercase "s," it refers to your own human spirit. When the emphasis is on the humanity of Jesus, you will see "Jesus Christ," and when the emphasis is on the deity of Jesus, He will be referred to as "Christ Jesus."

The fact that the Old Covenant of law is obsolete certainly fits with Christ's statement about the law being preached until John the Baptist. The gospel of the kingdom is not under the law; it is an aspect of the New Covenant.

Jesus Christ declares Himself to be not under the law in Matthew 17:24–27 (NKJV):

"When they had come to Capernaum, those who received the temple tax came to Peter and said, 'Does your Teacher not pay the temple tax?'

He said, 'Yes.' And when he had come into the house, Jesus anticipated him, saying, 'What do you think, Simon? From whom do the kings of the earth take customs or taxes, from their sons or from strangers?'

Peter said to Him, 'From strangers.' Jesus said to him, 'Then the sons are free.

'Nevertheless, lest we offend them, go to the sea, cast in a hook, and take the fish that comes up first. And when you have opened its mouth, you will find a piece of money; take that and give it to them for Me and you.'"

The temple tax was paid in obedience to the law of Moses. No one under the law was exempt from it. Since Jesus said that both He and Peter were exempt, it meant that they were neither under the law nor subject to the law. Jesus paid the tax—not because the law says He must, but to avoid offending those Jews who would not understand, as he did not want to be a stumbling block to them.

Christians of the New Covenant certainly understand that the church has financial needs, mainly to support the poor and to get the gospel out. How did Paul the apostle, who was a teacher of teachers and understood the Mosaic law, explain the Christian's obligation in his second letter to the Corinthians?

Paul, who saw himself as a minister of the New Covenant, stated that the law kills but the Spirit gives life (2 Corinthians 3:6). That which has been done away with (the law) is not as glorious as the New Covenant which remains (2 Corinthians 3:11 NKJV): "For if what is passing away was glorious, what remains is much more glorious."

Paul implored his Christian brothers not to receive the grace of God in vain because they withheld their affection for him (2 Corinthians 6:1–12). Paul was trying to persuade them to change from their traditional Judaism to the New Covenant, so he was asking them to please open their hearts to him. He cited the example of the Macedonian churches, who had given generously even to the point of self-sacrifice. This was Paul's appeal for a relief fund for Jerusalem, which was going through a famine.

In 2 Corinthians 8:1–5, Paul was saying, in essence, "Look, the Macedonians have made a financial sacrifice; can't you do likewise?" Remember: Our omniscient God always sees the heart amount, not the actual amount.

Note: Paul did not make a command or state a percentage; instead, he asked for a turning of the heart. All support for the body of Christ throughout the world and your local church should be offerings only based on sincere love and not from compulsion. Paul reminded them that Christ had become poor for their sakes. The implication is that the Corinthians should make financial sacrifices in return (2 Corinthians 8:8–9).

Paul was aiming for equality in their giving. That means you should not give money from your credit card if you cannot pay it back at the end of the month. God does not want borrowed money. Paul wanted to make sure that this new way of financing God's work was not from compulsion or from giving grudgingly, and so he repeated it in 2 Corinthians 9:5–7: God rewards generosity, generously.

Another good example that causes people to praise God and puts the gospel in a favourable light is 2 Corinthians 9:12–14. This was a collection for the poor in Judea, but Paul said nothing about tithing. Paul appealed to the New Covenant way of giving; Christ had made many sacrifices for them, so they ought to make some sacrifices to help one another. When Paul asked them to lay aside a certain amount on the first day of the week, it was for famine relief; it had nothing to do with the modern-day teaching of the tithe, which is so often preached in a lot of churches today.

In asking for their offering, Paul was also making a financial sacrifice; he had a right to receive financial support himself, but instead, he was asking for the offering to be given to others. Paul had not asked for any financial support from Corinth (2 Corinthians 11:7–11 and 12:13–16). Paul was supported by Macedonians and did not burden the Corinthians.

Paul was a tent maker and so worked to support himself, as well as taking support from those who could afford to provide for him, but he did not take from the people of Corinth, as he did not want to be a burden. When we see our brothers, who belong to the body of Christ but are not in our congregation, we will be more likely to share our resources because of Paul's example to us.

Paul had a right to be supported by the Corinthians, but he did not use it.

1 Corinthians 9:3–15 tells us about our Christian duty to give financial support to the gospel. Throughout his appeal, Paul does not cite any laws of tithing. He says that priests received benefits from their work in the temple in 2 Corinthians 9:13, but he does not cite any percentage.

Let's have a look at the fundamental scriptures of the New Covenant that we Christians now enjoy. We can see that the law has gone from external rules to the hidden man of the heart. Now our spirit, led by the Holy Spirit, will communicate with our soul (mind), as seen in these scriptures. Hebrews 8:6–13 shows that the law of Moses could declare God's holy standard, but it could never provide the power needed for obedience. Sinful people need a new heart and a new disposition within, and this is just what the New Covenant provides. Ezekiel prophesied that this day would come in Ezekiel 36:26–27 (NKJV):

"I will give you a new heart and put a new spirit within you; I will take the heart of stone out of your flesh and give you a heart of flesh.

I will put My Spirit within you and cause you to walk in My Statutes, and you will keep My judgments and do them."

The law was external; God's demands were written on tablets of stone, and now they are written in our heart. The Holy Spirit gave me this truth: He said, "Stewart, I see the heart amount, not the amount in your hand." I was determined from that time to be Spirit led in all my finances.

Note: It is unfortunate that many Christians think they are saved by grace but must then fulfil their Christian life according to the Old Testament law. They want the New Covenant for salvation, but the Old Testament law for prosperity (combined with some offerings). Now, all offerings are from the heart. We do not become holy people by trying to obey God's law in our own power. It is by yielding to the Holy Spirit within that we fulfil the righteousness of the law, and this is entirely by grace:

"There is therefore now no condemnation to those who are in Christ Jesus, who do not walk according to the flesh, but according to the Spirit.

For the law of the Spirit of life in Christ Jesus has made me free from the law of sin and death.

For what the law could not do in that it was weak through the flesh, God did by sending His own son in the likeness of sinful flesh, on account of sin: He condemned sin in the flesh,

that the righteous requirement of the law might be fulfilled in us who do not walk according to the flesh but according to the Spirit" (Romans 8:1–4 NKJV).

Tithing was not mentioned in any of Paul's letters to the churches. If this was to be a universal principle to all New Covenant prosperity, he surely would have mentioned it.

We can clearly see workers deserve to be paid; Jesus said that in Luke 10:7 (NKJV). Jesus said, "And remain in the same house, eating and drinking such things as they give, for the labourer is worthy of his wages. Do not go from house to house."

See also 1 Timothy 5:17–18 and 1 Corinthians 9:14.

The source of this income is offerings from Christians and is not a tax, as is the tithe. Elders, especially those who preach and teach, should be respected and honoured financially. Jesus also commented that those who preach the gospel should receive their living from the gospel.

Paul made tents to support himself, just like ministers of the gospel can go out to work in a secular job to complement a shortfall in offerings and not insist on a 10 percent levy on their gross income. We can now give with love and gratitude because of what Christ has done. He has become our firstfruits, and we are the harvest to follow.

Note: There are many promises of rewards for generosity in the New Covenant.

Christian Giving

Paul encouraged Christians to excel in the gracious act of giving for the relief fund for the poor Jewish Christians in Jerusalem. Lush, bountiful giving is a true mark of grace. The Lord of all glory, by His poverty, made us rich and became one of us. Grace is the foundation of all New Testament prosperity. All giving should hinge on why we give; it is all to do with the heart attitude. True giving is a joy, in contrast with giving begrudgingly.

Note: The Greek word translated "new" means new in quality, not new in time. The New Covenant is of such quality, it will never have to be replaced. It is eternal, and Jesus is now the High Priest; that is why it is a new and better covenant. While the Old Testament was in force, the ministry of the priests was ordained by God (that is, the practise of the tithe was perfectly proper). In AD 70, the city of Jerusalem was destroyed by the tenth Roman legion under General Titus; the Jews have not had a temple or priesthood to serve them ever since. Christians now live under the New Covenant, and the laws are written into their hearts. Spirit-led giving is the new standard:

"For this is the covenant that I will make with the house of Israel after those days, says the LORD: I will put My laws in their mind and write them on their hearts; and I will be their God, and they shall be My people" (Hebrews 8:10 NKJV).

We are not depending on a high priest on earth, who annually visits the Holy of Holies in a temporary sanctuary. We depend on the heavenly High Priest, Jesus, who has entered once and for all into the eternal sanctuary. There He represents us before God, and He always will.

When grace abounds, there is a lot of love and therefore not a lot of need for laws. If people operated out of love, they would not break God's laws.

God did not give us the law to make us good. He gave the law to expose our sin. The law was actually called the ministry of death, and shortly after the law was given, three thousand people died. Interestingly, in the day of grace after the Holy Spirit was poured out at Pentecost, three thousand people were added to the church.

God's law was never given to establish a relationship; it was given to unregenerate man to show him how he should behave. This required six hundred laws, a living code, and the Ten Commandments.

Under the New Covenant, God does not demand a change in your lifestyle before you accept Him. So when it comes to your labels, current or post, God is slow to judge and more than willing to deliver. If grace had limits, the behaviour of King David would not have been forgiven, as spoken by Nathan, the prophet.

Romans 5:20 (NKJV) says, "Moreover the law entered that the offense might abound. But where sin abounded, grace abounded much more."

Paul explained that we no longer live under the requirements of the law (Romans 6:14), and the Apostle John made the same point in John 1:17. Neither John nor Paul meant that God's grace was not active in the Old Testament because God has always dealt graciously with His people. We can now see the overwhelming power of God's grace was shown to us by what Jesus did for us at Calvary.

Many missionaries throughout the world are in need of financial help, so we should certainly look outside of our own lives and be generous. We have an obligation to help our brothers in Christ, and when we give ourselves to the Lord and grow in Christ, we will give generously.

Jesus mentioned different amounts to different people when it came to giving money (for example, the religious rich man in Luke 18:22).

Riches were his whole life; he was spiritually unfruitful, and Jesus knew that only 100 percent giving was going to set this man free. In Luke 8:14, Jesus warned about storing up wealth for self without being rich towards God. The rich man described in Luke 12:16–21 would have done well to have given the excess from his crops to the poor and needy, instead of building bigger barns to store it all for himself.

Here is a wonderful promise in Luke 12:33 (NKJV); when we use wealth to help others, we gain treasure in heaven: "Sell what you have and give alms; provide yourselves money bags which do not grow old, a treasure in the heavens that does not fail, where no thief approaches nor moth destroys."

Money, even though it is meant to be a medium of exchange which superseded the barter system, does compete for your allegiance. It tempts us to seek our own desires rather than the needs of God's kingdom. You cannot serve two masters (Luke 16:13); it is imperative to focus on the gospel and make money serve you. Just be a conduit to get this wonderful good news out.

Very few gospel entrepreneurs are rich because a consecrated life is required, where your focus is kingdom building. Generally speaking, it is harder for rich people to have their names written down in the Lamb's Book of Life and enter the kingdom of God because their focus is on money:

"And when Jesus saw that he became very sorrowful, He said, 'How hard it is for those who have riches to enter the kingdom of God!

'For it is easier for a camel to go through the eye of a needle than for a rich man to enter the kingdom of God'" (Luke 18:24–25 NKJV).

There are exceptions, and in the section on patrons of the gospel, we will see men and women who financially supported great men of the gospel. The bottom line is this: Christians need to share their resources and blessings with others and support the preaching of the gospel.

We have seen the three different tithes in the Old Testament. The New Covenant does not specify a percentage. For some people, 3 percent may be too much, and for others, 25 percent would be affordable. Offerings should be given to the church for its collective work of preaching the gospel.

The Old Covenant required simple percentages. Everyone knew how much was required. The New Covenant requires more soul searching, more training for the conscience, more selfless love for others, more faith, more voluntary sacrifice, and less compulsion. It certainly tests our values, what we treasure most, and the motive of the heart.

Generosity Eliminates Poverty

Paul writes in his second letter to the Corinthians how the grace given to the Macedonians by God resulted in abundant joy when they gave to the relief fund for Jerusalem:

"Moreover, brethren, we make known to you the grace of God bestowed on the churches of Macedonia:

that in a great trial of affliction the abundance of their joy and their deep poverty abounded in the riches of their liberality" (2 Corinthians 8:1–2 NKJV).

In his heart, Paul hoped this would inspire the Corinthians to respond to God's grace in a similar way. I have noticed in my Christian walk that when I go and help others, my joy increases. Look again at 2 Corinthians 8:2; their response shows something quite beyond the natural world of selfish humanity, something that cannot be explained by the values of this world.

Note: The amazing fact is when you combine poverty and joy, you get rich generosity. This is superior to the Old Testament percentage-based giving, as seen in 2 Corinthians 8:3 (NKJV):

"For I bear witness that according to their ability, yes, and beyond their ability, they were freely willing."

If this wasn't amazing enough, in 2 Corinthians 8:4, they in their poverty were begging Paul for an opportunity to give more than was reasonable. Such a demonstration of grace was a testimony to their Spirit-empowered love for other people, and this grace is available to us also. They accomplished this out-of-this-world giving by giving themselves first to the Lord and then to the need of the Corinthians:

"And not only as we had hoped, but they first gave themselves to the Lord and then to us by the will of God" (2 Corinthians 8:5 NKJV).

The result was a work of grace in their hearts, and they were happy to do it. We now go from a formula to a relationship with the Holy Spirit in our giving; we experience a freedom and see the favour of God on our lives.

Paul said you excel in faith, speech, and knowledge; see that you also excel in the grace of giving (2 Corinthians 8:7). He wanted the Corinthians to excel in generosity because that is an expression of Godly love, and love is what is most important. He knew that no matter how much a person may give, it wouldn't do any good if the attitude was resentful (1 Corinthians 13:3 NKJV):

"And though I bestow all my goods to feed the poor, and though I give my body to be burned, but have not love, it profits me nothing."

Jesus Is Our Standard, Our Secure Foundation

True grace is not found in what the Corinthians boasted about; it is measured by the perfect standard of Jesus Christ, who gave His life for all (2 Corinthians 8:9 NKJV):

"For you know the grace of our Lord Jesus Christ, that though He was rich, yet for your sakes He became poor, that you through His poverty might become rich."

In 1998, when I started to be led in all my giving, I was praying one morning, and the Holy Spirit said to give $50 to Janet (not her real name). She had been crying to the Lord because she had no money to celebrate her birthday. She asked God to tell someone to give her $50. I spoke to her privately when I met her at church; she was so happy that God had answered her prayer.

You Do Your Best, and God Will Do the Rest

When our daughter was overseas with Youth With a Mission (YWAM), she needed $5,000 for her studies; Merilyn did fundraisers and put as much of her own pay into it as she could, but when the time came to pay, she was $2,000 short. She said, "Well, God, I've done the best I can; who has the $2,000 I need?" He showed her a vision of our worship leader at church, and she said to the Lord, "You will have to tell her, because I can't ask her for it."

On Sunday at church, the worship leader came running up to Merilyn; she was very excited that she had heard from the Lord. She said God had just told her to give $2,000 for our daughter.

Merilyn said, "Oh, thank you. I am so glad you are excited to give it. I sure am glad to receive it," and then explained to her all about our effort to raise the money and how we had a shortfall and asked the

Lord who had the money. We did show our appreciation afterwards with a special dinner for our very generous friend.

I know God's faithful people have problems, trials, and even poverty, and yet, because Jesus lives in us, we can be rich in generosity. We can excel in giving because joy in Christ can overflow in us to be a blessing to others.

Note: Jesus was willing to be impoverished for us, and in this New Covenant, we are called to give up things in this world, to live by different values, and to serve Him by serving others.

Joy and Generosity

Paul explained that what you start, you should finish:

"And in this I give advice: It is to your advantage not only to be doing what you began and were desiring to do a year ago;

but now you also must complete the doing of it; that as there was a readiness to desire it, so there also may be a completion out of what you have" (2 Corinthians 8:10–11 NKJV).

Paul wanted generosity to be voluntary; as I mentioned before, you will receive God's joy. He states only to give within your ability. Remember: Humanity looks on the outside, and God looks on the inside of you.

Paul continues his exhortations in 2 Corinthians 9:2 (NKJV):

"For I know your willingness, about which I boast of you to the Macedonians, that Achaia was ready a year ago; and your zeal has stirred up the majority."

Note: This cheerfulness does not mean hilarity or laughter. It means that because Christ is in us, we enjoy sharing what we have with others; it gives us great satisfaction when we bless others. Love and grace work in our hearts in such a way that little by little, a life of giving becomes a greater and greater pleasure to us.

The Greater Blessing

Here Paul speaks about rewards; just like the secular work force has a reward system in some industries, God has a wonderful reward system, so after they have been encouraged to give from the heart, graciously and willingly, Paul pens the following, under the direction of the Holy Spirit:

"And God is able to make all grace abound toward you, that you, always having all sufficiency in all things, may have an abundance for every good work" (2 Corinthians 9:8 NKJV).

Note: When God gave extra grace to the Macedonian churches, they had less money than before but more joy. Now any sane person, if forced to choose, would rather have poverty with joy than wealth without joy. Joy is the greater blessing, and God gives us the greater blessing. Some Christians even get both joy and wealth, but they are also given the responsibility to use both to serve others.

In 2 Corinthians 9:9 (NKJV), Paul quotes from the Old Testament: "As it is written: 'He has dispersed abroad, He has given to the poor; His righteousness endures forever.'"

This gift of righteousness (right standing with God) is the greatest gift, and this lasts forever. God gives us the best possible gift.

God Rewards Generosity

"Now may He who supplies seed to the sower, and bread for food, supply and multiply the seed you have sown and increase the fruits on your righteousness" (2 Corinthians 9:10 NKJV).

The bottom line is, God blesses you more, so you have more to give. To the person who is using God's gifts to serve, He will give more. Sometimes, He gives in kind (grain for grain, money for money), but not always. Sometimes, He blesses us with joy immeasurable in return for sacrificial giving. He always gives the best.

Note: Paul did say that the Corinthians would have all that they needed. For what purpose? So they would abound in every good work (2 Corinthians 9:12). God's gifts are to be used and not hidden or kept to ourselves.

Those who are rich are to become rich in good works:

"Let them do good, that they be rich in good works, ready to give, willing to share" (1 Timothy 6:18 NKJV).

Trials and Tribulations

God did not promise an easy life. There are still many people being martyred for their faith. The New Covenant did not promise a comfortable life for anyone. People who live in Australia should be very grateful. The Human Index ranks Australia second in the world in standard of living, after Norway. We enjoy a good standard of living and are, for the most part, kind and generous people who will empathise and help where help is needed.

In October 2014, Merilyn and I experienced the grace of our Lord Jesus Christ. We were driving to visit our friends who had just moved to Beverley. The trip from Perth should have gotten us there for lunch at 12.30 p.m. The GPS had other ideas, and we ended up stuck in a bog in the National Forest. We left the car and walked for seven hours; finally, at 9.15 p.m., we lay down on the roadside, as we were tired, and it was so dark that we couldn't see the track. We both experienced a supernatural peace as we sang and prayed our way through the forest.

We had only been resting for a little while, maybe fifteen minutes, when we saw headlights coming, and we leaped off the road, while waving and shouting for the driver to stop and help us. There were three beekeepers in a four-wheel drive; they said they don't usually stop for people in the forest because of the risk. Something, we know it was God answering our prayers, made them stop to see what we wanted. We asked them to call the RAC to help us, but they said that they had the equipment to get us out. They took us back to our car and pulled it out of the bog. They set off through the forest and had us follow them to show us the direction back home. We thank God for those beekeepers, who were so very generous and went out of their way to save us from harm that night.

God has demonstrated His love to us that even while we were sinners, He sent His Son to die for us. Remember: We are not sinners because we sin; we sin because we are sinners. Grace enables God to change us from the inside, and we start to think and act as He thinks. Now, since God has already demonstrated His love for us, we can confidently trust Him to take care of us, as He did for Merilyn and I in the forest that night. We are not only His children, but we are His friends, so we don't have to be anxious about lacking anything:

"And my God shall supply all your need according to His riches in glory by Christ Jesus" (Philippians 4:19 NKJV).

The Harvest of Praise

Let's continue with the Corinthians; Paul tells them about their financial and material prosperity. He is reminding them in 2 Corinthians 9:11–12 that their generosity is not just a humanitarian effort; it has theological results. People come to realise that God works through people. God lays it on the hearts of those who have to give; that is the New Covenant way in which God gets His work done.

In Matthew 6:26 (NKJV), we see Christ's message, which reveals our worth to God:

"Look at the birds of the air, for they neither sow nor reap nor gather into barns; yet your heavenly Father feeds them. Are you not of more value than they?"

God cares for His children not because they are giving to the church, as that would be a works program (despite some financial teachings to the contrary). The Father cares for us because we are His. Jesus came to earth to redeem us from sin and paid a huge price for us. We are valuable to Him.

New Covenant Prophecy

The Lord said in Jeremiah 31:31 that the New Covenant would not be like the Old Covenant and that the children of Israel broke the covenant. God is like a husband to those in the covenant and implies that Israel is like an unfaithful wife.

Jeremiah 31:33 (NKJV) says, "But this is the covenant that I will make with the house of Israel after those days, says the LORD: I will put My law in their minds, and write it on their hearts; and I will be their God, and they shall be My people."

The Old Covenant was written on stone; the New Covenant is written in the hearts of people. The Old Covenant was an external law; the New Covenant is internal and gives people a Christ-like nature. God said that He will be their God and that they will be His people. This implies that the New Covenant people will experience a closer, more intimate relationship with God than those under the Old Covenant

Most of the Israelites did not know God personally and needed to be taught by the kings, prophets, and priests. All people under the New Covenant have a personal relationship with God because Jesus Christ took our sin and sickness for us on the cross. Jeremiah 31:34.

Giving for the Gospel

When we give financially towards the gospel and ministry, the principle is still the same today as it was when the Bible was written. We give to famine relief, provide for workers who preach the gospel, and support the pastoral ministers. The finances enable the church to provide a building where people can learn about the Bible and have fellowship, and newcomers can receive salvation.

God rewards those who give generously for their sacrifices, faith, and diligence. We all share in the benefits of giving financially to the church, and our contributions also help to provide for others in the body of Christ who are in need.

Money and Worship

Many churches take up offerings for special causes and to relieve the suffering of others who may be experiencing famine or homelessness or persecution. It is a form of worship to God to give gladly. Generosity gladdens the heart and gives a sense of power to be able to change and better someone else's life, and it also pleases God.

Offerings Express Love for God

Jesus went to the cross for us, He gave us everything. Giving back to Him is a form of worship, it is a way to express our gratitude and love. The church relies on our offerings as an important part of the budget, but our giving is not a response from an obligation to the law. It is a commitment and devotion to further the work of God, to spread His word and reach out into all the world.

Three Reasons to Give

When we give from the heart we are putting treasures in Heaven for eternity. God does bless us while we are still here on earth too:

God blesses those who give (Luke 18:29–30).

God commands his people to give (Acts 20:35).

The church needs money to serve the members. In 2 Corinthians 8:1–5, Paul wanted a change of heart; he wanted the people to give themselves to the Lord and then to others. Therefore, their giving would be done in love.

Paul Asks for Generosity

The Corinthians could not give more than they had, and they were not being asked to impoverish themselves. Paul is appealing to the rich to share their abundance with those in need.

Paul Had a Right to Financial Support

In 1 Corinthians 9:14, Jesus said that those who preach the gospel should receive their living from the gospel. Therefore, people who believe in the gospel should contribute towards the living expenses of those who preach. It is a duty, and there is a reward.

In Luke 12:21, Jesus warns about greed and the danger of storing up wealth. We need to be "rich toward God" and guard our heart (Luke 12:34). Remember, grace is not ours to earn; it is God's to give. Grace not only extends to our provision; it also covers our salvation.

We will go to the same heaven as the first martyr, Stephen. Is that fair? No, it's God's grace. Some people say that the thief only went to the grave and stayed there. But the word "Paradise" (in the Greek, *Paradeisos*) means "the place of future happiness."

The ultimate prosperity would be a prosperity that is guaranteed beyond grace. A place in heaven where there is no crime or sickness, but incredible joy and peace, and a mansion to live in that was only made possible by the sacrificial death of Jesus. This gave God the latitude to grant the Sauls of this world, and the last-minute converts, the same eternal home.

You are not saved by your good works, but you are saved for good works. Grace plus anything added to it is anything but grace. For example, the Judaisers said to the new Christians that they can have faith in Jesus Christ plus obey the law of Moses. This would make life frustrating and barren, but to live by grace through faith gives one a free and fulfilling Christian life.

The church is most appealing when the message of grace is preached. Grace is never just enough; grace is always more than enough. The difference between mercy and grace is, mercy is not giving you what you deserve, but grace is giving you what you don't deserve. It is because of grace that God chose to clean up what we messed up. God's approval is not based on your performance but on Christ's performance.

You cannot get your salvation by works (Ephesians 2:8–9).

You cannot get your healing by works (1 Peter 2:24).

You cannot get your prosperity by works (2 Corinthians 8:9).

Pray and ask God what He would like you to do to prosper the kingdom. Whatever He tells you to do, do it! Grace is God's part; faith is our part (Matthew 6:31–33).

The Old Testament law required people to live in perfect obedience and showed up their sin nature and the need for a saviour. In the New Testament, living by grace is relying on Christ and His perfect life of obedience, drawing each day on the power of the Holy Spirit.

We must stop trying to mingle the Old Covenant with the New Covenant; this was made poignant by the writer of Hebrews. God took away the first Covenant to establish a new and better second Covenant (Hebrews 10:9).

Note: This does not only apply to our salvation through the wonderful (although costly and painful) sacrifice of Jesus; it also means we go from formulas to relationship. So which is better: a tour book (law) or a tour guide (Holy Spirit)?

Why do we now need God's grace to get through this fallen world?

"Therefore, as through one man's offense judgment came to all men, resulting in condemnation, even so through one Man's righteous act the free gift came to all men, resulting in justification of life.

For as by one man's disobedience many were made sinners, so also by one Man's obedience many will be made righteous" (Romans 5:18–19 NKJV).

The book of Romans explains that the Old Covenant or old realm is ruled by death, sin, the law, and sinful nature. The New Covenant (new realm) is characterised by life, righteous living, grace, and the Holy Spirit. People's destinies are controlled by the realm they are living in.

Note: The best thing the law did was to identify sin and intensify our guilt. The emphasis is not on what we do for God (Old Covenant); instead, it is on what God (through Jesus Christ) has done for us. Therefore, seeing grace as an undeserved privilege, rather than an exclusive right, keeps you humble. God exalts the humble but resists the proud. You are either depending on deserved favour through your self-efforts or grace (unmerited favour), based on what Jesus has done for you.

His unmerited favour will cause you to enjoy success beyond your natural intelligence, qualifications, and ability. It is the presence of the Lord in your life that makes you a success. It is not what you have, it is who you have that makes all the difference. When God's presence is made manifest in your life, that is when glory shines forth in you. Your focus must always be on Jesus and not on your situation. He will carry you through and bring you out into victory.

Look at the grace on Joseph when he was in charge of Potiphar's house (Potiphar was the captain of Pharaoh's Egyptian guards):

"And his master saw that the LORD was with him and that the LORD made all he did to prosper in his hand" (Genesis 39:3 NKJV).

Note: When you start doing God's will and depending on God's divine favour, you will begin to experience the "Jesus" kind of results. Remember, without Him we cannot, and without us, He will not. All works, no matter how good they are and how pretty they look, are in vain if they do not flow from grace. Grace says you have nothing to give, nothing to earn, nothing to pay.

The word of God says that if you give to charity in secret, God will reward you openly, so keep the extent of your giving to yourself.

Essence of God's Grace

If our greatest need had been for information, God would have sent us an educator.

Jesus waits patiently for you to trust on His unmerited favour, so stop struggling in your own attempts to somehow deserve His favour, and just depend on Him. Ask God for ideas, and He will give them to you, and then act on them.

Let's see how God deals with us from the point of relationship. As a parent, how would you teach your child character and patience? By putting disease or sickness on them? Of course not. Or would you teach humility by poverty? No. So your heavenly Father is not going to do it, either. If your heart is for God's cause (kingdom building) and not your cause, you will prosper:

"Let them shout for joy and be glad, who favour my righteous cause; and let them say continually, 'Let the LORD be magnified, who has pleasure in the prosperity of His servant'" (Psalm 35:27 NKJV).

God is not against you having money and material things; He is against money having you. Knowing Jesus is your success and makes you safe for success. Prosperity is not just finances, wealth, income, or investments; it extends to excellent health, friends, family, and good relationships. Love should have no conditions; extend grace to others as Jesus Christ has shown you abundant grace. Share your time and resources with others and thereby show the love of Christ.

Note: Jesus loves us despite our flawed natures. King David, who was after God's heart, still failed. He committed adultery with Bathsheba and arranged for her husband Uriah to be placed in the front of the battle, where he was subsequently killed, along with his army. Under the law, even the best failed; under grace, even the worst can be saved. Grace also covers our salvation, not just prosperity.

Let us be a people who will not depend on our own wisdom, might, and riches, but rather let our dependence be on understanding and knowing Jesus:

"Thus says the LORD: 'Let not the wise man glory in his wisdom, let not the mighty man glory in his might, nor let the rich man glory in his riches;

But let him who glories glory in this, that he understands and knows Me, that I am the LORD, exercising loving kindness, judgement, and righteousness in the earth. For in these I delight,' says the LORD" (Jeremiah 9:23–24 NKJV).

The bottom line is to rest in Him. The more you focus on beholding Jesus in all His loveliness, the less you struggle to earn things by your own merit, and the more you become safe for greater success in your life.

The wonderful thing about grace is, your past will not determine the future God has for you. Now what you appreciate, appreciates value in your own eyes. Your righteousness in Christ is your right to God's unmerited favour:

"For He made Him who knew no sin to be sin for us, that we might become the righteousness of God in Him" (2 Corinthians 5:21 NKJV).

Our righteousness is a result of Jesus's work, and we can only receive His righteousness through His unmerited favour: "I do not set aside the grace of God; for if righteousness comes through the law, then Christ died in vain" (Galatians 2:21 NKJV).

The law was only a temporary measure put in place until Jesus comes:

"But before faith came, we were kept under guard by the law, kept for the faith which would afterward be revealed.

Therefore the law was our tutor to bring us to Christ, that we might be justified by faith.

But after faith has come, we are no longer under a tutor" (Galatians 3:23–25 NKJV).

We go from strict law keeping to a Spirit-led relationship with the Holy Spirit. Now that grace has come through Jesus, we are no longer under the law. In the Old Covenant law, you had to do something to get favour; with grace, you get favour before you do something.

The New Testament will herald in a New Covenant (agreement), so the New Covenant supersedes the Old Covenant. Now, by calling this covenant new, He has made the first one obsolete, and what is obsolete and aging will soon disappear (Hebrews 8:13).

The apostle said, "Ye are not under the law but under grace" (Romans 6:14). In short, why should anyone remain under the law's curse, who is not under the law? To do so would be the same as putting a man in prison after he had been proven innocent and the court had justified him from the charge.

Let's take a look at the New Covenant benefits of grace that was written by the Apostle Paul in Romans 8:1–4 (NKJV):

"There is therefore now no condemnation to those who are in Christ Jesus, who do not walk according to the flesh, but according to the Spirit.

For the law of the Spirit of life in Christ Jesus has made me free from the law of sin and death.

For what the law could not do in that it was weak through the flesh, God did by sending His own son in the likeness of sinful flesh, on account of sin: He condemned sin in the flesh,

that the righteous requirement of the law might be fulfilled in us who do not walk according to the flesh but according to the Spirit."

If our greatest need had been financial, God would have sent us an economist; if our need had been pleasure, God would have sent us an entertainer. But our greatest need was forgiveness, so God sent us a Saviour.

Of all the internal killers ready to pounce on grace, none is more powerful than pride. Pride gives strength to sin because it will not let you repent and receive your much-needed forgiveness. Paul, who was a teacher of teachers, a Pharisee of Pharisees, is our magnificent example; he accepted grace because he no longer put confidence in the flesh, that is, in his own natural ability.

The foundation, of course, is *love*. Love that goes upward is worship, love that goes outward is affection, and love that reaches down is *grace*. Make grace your foundation and graciousness the badge you wear. The pure definition of grace is, to extend favour or kindness to one who does not deserve it and can never earn it.

God's presence is with you. The Holy Spirit is always present to direct you, to guide you, to lead you into becoming more Christ-like and to make you a success in every endeavour you undertake.

Look at the grace that was shown towards Paul in 1 Corinthians 15:9–10; before he converted to Christianity, he used to kill Christians. Grace is undeserved, and yet it is unconditional. The dreadful tyranny of performing in order to please someone is over. Paul's statement shows it up well in Galatians 2:19 (NKJV): "For I through the law died to the law that I might live to God."

The law demands from man, but grace (unmerited favour) points you to your sufficiency in Christ; it imparts to man. The law is about what you must do, but grace is all about what Jesus has done. The law makes you self-conscious, but grace makes you Christ-conscious.

A church must not slip in and out of the two covenants; what man calls "balance," Jesus calls a mixture. Jesus did not come to give us more laws; He came to give us His unmerited favour, which is the truth. This truth that you know will truly set you free from legalism.

The amazing thing was that the Abrahamic Covenant was grace, and then the Mosaic Covenant was law. After the resurrection of Jesus came the New Covenant: grace (unmerited favour). The irony is the more you try to keep the law by your own efforts, the more it will bring forth what it was designed to bring forth (like switching the light on); it shows up your failings and sins. It shows that you need a saviour; it points to Jesus.

Note: Grace forgives your sin, but it does not erase the scars that accompany sin. The ramifications could stay with you for the rest of your life, as it was with King David of Israel. How we live depends on the master we choose.

Guiding grace is refusing to dictate to others, and this allows the Lord freedom to direct people's lives. If you are unsure how to act in a situation, the book of James says we can ask God for wisdom, and He will give it to us (James 1:5).

"For sin shall not have dominion over you, for you are not under law but under grace" (Romans 6:14 NKJV).

Grace lives above the demands of human opinion and breaks free from legalistic regulations. You will have noticed more authors are writing about grace now. The new movement of grace will someday sweep across every continent, and the long-standing will of the Old

Covenant that has kept people in bondage for centuries will come tumbling down. Tens of thousands will say, "Free at last."

Complaining was not punished under the Abrahamic Covenant in the wilderness, as they were in a grace period (unmerited favour), but they were punished under the Mosaic Covenant (the giving of the law), based on their performance.

The Old Covenant of law was not God's best for Israel; they asked for it when they boasted in their ability to be blessed, based on their own works: "We will do everything that the Lord has commanded" Exodus 24:3 (HCSB).

No hewn stone (Exodus 20:25 NKJV) equals no human effort. You cannot add to Jesus's sacrifice, nor can you deserve His favour by depending on your obedience to the law. Humanity cannot gain access to God's unmerited favour by his own steps.

All five offerings of the Old Covenant (burnt, peace, meat, sin, trespass) all point to one perfect offering: Jesus Christ on the cross.

Isn't it amazing that Jesus, our perfect payment, cleansed our lifetime of sins, and now we can walk in newness of life with the righteousness of the Lamb of God? No other religion offers such a wonderful promise and act of grace.

The commandments were never given to stop sin; they were given to expose sin. The strength of sin is the law. Christ drank from the cup of God's wrath, so you could drink from the cup of God's grace. The law has been nailed to the cross. In the same way that you can't use a mirror to clean the dirt that it has exposed off your face, you cannot use the law to remove the sins that it has exposed and make you holy. The law has no power to make us holy.

In each realm, the Old Covenant and the New Covenant is headed by a man who represents its constituents. The old realm of sin and death (spiritual death; we all die physically) is headed by Adam, the first man. The new realm, the New Covenant, which is of forgiveness and life (God's kind of life: *Zoe*), is headed by Christ. Our human nature belongs to the old realm and is represented by Adam the first man, whose sin and death controls the destiny of all people.

When you are overflowing with God's love, you will fulfil the law effortlessly, without even trying. The children of God are set free from the bondage of legalism. Galatians 3:13 states that all believers are redeemed from the curse of the law through Jesus's finished work, but when a believer rejects God's grace and depends on his own works to be blessed, he falls back under the curse of the law.

Galatians 5:4 (NKJV) says, "You have become estranged from Christ, you who attempt to be justified by law; you have fallen from grace."

Nobody can keep the law perfectly. The moment you fail in one part of the law, you are guilty of failing in all of it. Jesus had to die on the cross to redeem us from the curse of the law, not the curse of sin. The problem is that man relies on his own efforts to prosper. When you ask for God's plan, it is automatically blessed. God gave us the strategy to buy and sell gold and to buy the investment home, and He has blessed it, so we have made a profit.

The more righteousness-conscious you are; the more blessings will follow you. Trust in God's undeserved favour in your life. The heart of the problem is the human heart. The answer is not behaviour modification but inward heart transformation.

Note: Fear is not the opposite of faith; works are.

So we see a man is not justified by the works of the law but by faith in Jesus Christ. This applies to salvation, divine healing, and prosperity. We are redeemed from the threefold curse of the law: eternal damnation, sickness, and poverty (Galatians 2:15–16).

The law is about doing, whereas faith is about speaking. It is not faith until you speak it. The reassuring thing is even if you fail, your relationship with God is not broken because your failures have all been paid for at the cross.

The Differences between the Old Covenant of Law and the Covenant of Grace

Old Covenant of Law	New Covenant of Grace
God demanded man to be righteous.	God gave us righteousness through the finished work of Jesus. (Romans 4:5–7)
Your sin will be passed down to the third and fourth generation. (Exodus 20:5)	God will not remember your sin. (Hebrews 8:12 and 10:17)
Israel was blessed if they kept God's laws perfectly inwardly and outwardly. (Deuteronomy 28:13–14)	Jesus fulfilled all the requirements of the law. (Colossians 2:14)
Disobeying the commandments brought a curse. (Deuteronomy 28:15–16, 18, 20)	Jesus became a curse on the cross so believers can now enjoy blessings they don't deserve. (Galatians 3:13)
Annual blood sacrifice of animals.	Jesus's blood was shed once and for all.

Depending on self-effort is works, but God requires a heart transformation.	Admiration for Jesus produces an inner work of the heart, and that love motivates people to do good works. (2 Corinthians 3:18)
The law did not empower the children of Israel to stop sin in their lives.	Jesus empowers Christians not to sin but does not remove their free will.
The Israelites could not have an intimate relationship with God.	Believers enjoy an intimate relationship with God. (2 Corinthians 5:17)
Only the high priest could enter the Holy of Holies on the Day of Atonement. (Leviticus 16:2, 14)	The throne of grace is open to believers all the time because of Jesus's perfect Atonement. (Hebrews 4:16)
The Israelites were under the ministry of death. (2 Corinthians 3:7)	Jesus came to destroy the works of the enemy and to give believers abundant life. (2 Corinthians 3:6 and John 10:10)

God provides for us in many ways, but just sitting is not effective. God will bless your doing but not your sitting. Christians need to get out of the "mailbox mentality," where they give their 10 percent, and somehow God has to give them a cheque in the mail, or they expect someone to pay their debt for them. Yes, there have been incidents where someone is sincerely doing God's work and comes to the end of their money, and God has supernaturally provided.

Merilyn and I have seen God multiply our food when we had no money and also provided money for our daughter when she was in ministry with YWAM. What I am saying is that every financial emergency should not have to be a faith project. We had faithfully tithed and were just making it, getting further into debt, like thousands of other Christians.

When we started to be led by the Holy Spirit in our giving and asking for strategies, we turned our debt around. God gave Merilyn the idea to buy and sell gold, yet I was the financial consultant for Westpac. Since leaving Westpac, I have read thirty-two books on economics, yet Merilyn, who has not read any economic books, was given the strategy. I implemented the buying and selling of gold and also bought an investment home in Brisbane; this has given us financial independence. We have been led by the Holy Spirit in all our giving since 1998, and we will wait on direction from God whether to keep or sell our investment property and the right timing for that.

New Covenant of Grace

I retired in 2013, at sixty-four years of age, and have a great desire to help as many people as possible know the Lord Jesus Christ. I'd like them to see how blessed it is to live the Christian life, to understand the Bible, and to live the abundant life that Jesus obtained for us on the cross.

Jesus will cause you to reign over every storm in your life. Righteousness is not based on your perfect performance; it is based on His perfect work. Jesus is the bread of life, and bread must be eaten fresh every day. So come into His presence with prayer every day.

Note: The gospel of grace is not a license to sin; on the contrary, it is the power that enables people not to sin. When you really love a person, you want to do your best for them, so when you come to love Jesus, you want to please Him. The secret of good success is found in meditating on and reading aloud God's word (from the Greek, *hagah*, to utter or mutter) in the light of the New Covenant of Grace.

In the New Covenant, we go from formula and laws to a relationship with God, so we have faith in God's grace. He is able to do exceedingly and abundantly more than we ever hoped or dreamed of. He is merciful and gracious and not judgemental.

Hebrews 4:16 (NKJV) says, "Let us therefore come boldly to the throne of grace, that we may obtain mercy and find grace to help in time of need."

Knowledge puffs up, but wisdom will make you humble and teachable. Wisdom is the skilful use of knowledge in daily living, reflected in our relationships with family, friends, work mates, and the general public. Wisdom will always lead you to the person of Jesus Christ and to the cross. We simply need God's wisdom to succeed in all areas of our life (Proverbs 4:7–9).

So we can now see grace extends to all three parts of man: spirit (from the Greek, *pneuma*), soul (from the Greek, *psyche*: mind, will, and emotions), and body (physical needs: food, shelter, and clothing). True prosperity is a grace-based foundation and covers the triune nature of man.

Note: Under the Old Covenant, the high priest was only allowed into the presence of God once a year, on the Day of Atonement. You and I have free and complete access into Jesus's presence anytime.

Man showed by his flawed nature that he could not keep the law of the Old Covenant, and so God made a New Covenant that was based entirely on the perfect work of Jesus. We need a saviour and have access by faith into this grace. Remember: Grace is God's part, and faith is our part. Nothing is too small for God, if it matters to you, it matters to God.

1 Peter 5:7 (NKJV) says, "Casting all your care upon Him, for He cares for you." When you put God's business first, He will take care of your business and your needs. Peter gave Jesus his boat to use, and in return, Jesus gave Peter a boatful of fish.

Grace has two sides: It is something to be received, and it is something to be extended (that is, to be forwarded on). There is a delightful paradox: The more you give yourself up to God, the freer you become.

Key Points to Bring a Balance to Grace and Faith

- Faith is your part; grace is God's part.
- Put your faith in the grace of God, not in your ability.
- If you try to find God by works, that is legalism. If you live wholly on faith and gratitude for what God has already done, that is grace.
- True Christianity comes from the inside out. A good heart attitude will change a person's actions.

The gift of salvation makes the poorest beggar a prince; missing this gift makes the wealthiest man a pauper. However, in the natural world, we are still rich when compared to the 980 million people who struggle to get enough to eat every day. If you rent a house and have a car, you are in the top 7 percent of the 7.2 billion (that is 504 million) people in the world. If you have a home and a car, you are in the top 5 percent of the 7.2 billion (that is 360 million) people.

Human love can only take us so far. The gift God gives and grace He grants us, first the power to receive love and then the power to give it. We simply come to the throne room of grace and ask God to "create in me a new heart and renew a right spirit (His Holy Spirit) within me. Lord, increase my love and compassion for all people," and He will.

When you love the weak and the sick, you do what God does every single moment. Dare we ask for grace if we refuse to give love? Jesus was God's model of a human being, ever honest in the midst of hypocrisy, relentlessly kind in a world of cruelty. His love and mercy never ceases.

Here is an excellent prayer for your community:

"Lord, you declare Yourself in Your word to be the Lord who provides; come and release Your provision for these people that Your name be hallowed in this community."

Note: You cannot put grace and law together. The secret for reigning in life lies with receiving everything that Jesus has accomplished for us on the cross. True wealth is the assurance that you know you have a mansion waiting for you in Heaven, which was bought by the precious blood of Jesus. He has given you the gift of righteousness:

"For if by the one man's offense death reigned through the one, much more those who receive abundance of grace and of the gift of righteousness will reign in life through the One, Jesus Christ" (Romans 5:17 NKJV).

The devil is very crafty; he has no problem with righteousness, but he wants to deceive you into pursuing your own righteousness through the law. There is nothing you can do that will make God love you more, and there is nothing you can do that will make Him love you less:

"For He made Him who knew no sin to be sin for us, that we might become the righteousness of God in Him" (2 Corinthians 5:21 NKJV).

You did nothing to become righteous, and Jesus did nothing to become sin. Weary and heavy laden are the requirements of the law. True grace makes Jesus the centre of everything.

Paul Describes the Glory of the New Covenant

"But if the ministry of death, written and engraved on stones, was glorious, so that the children of Israel could not look steadily at the face of Moses because of the glory of his countenance, which glory was passing away, how will the ministry of the Spirit not be more glorious?

For if the ministry of condemnation had glory, the ministry of righteousness exceeds much more in glory" (2 Corinthians 3:7–9 NKJV).

Fifty days after the first Passover, God gave the Ten Commandments at Mount Sinai, and three thousand people died (Exodus:15–28), but on the day of Pentecost on Mount Zion, three thousand people got saved, and the New Covenant church was born (Acts 2:41).

The law demands righteousness from sinful man, whereas grace imparts righteousness to sinful man. The law demands perfection but will not lift a finger to help. Grace imparts perfection and does everything for man through Jesus Christ, and all that man has to do is believe. Which do you think is more glorious: the ministry of death that demands, or the ministry of grace that imparts?

God gave the law to bring man to the end of himself, so that he would see his need for a saviour. The law which was given to all people before the cross, although holy, just, and good, had no power to make you and me holy. Why should we be told to go back to an inferior covenant with regard to salvation, healing, and prosperity?

The law always ministers condemnation; grace, on the other hand, always ministers righteousness. Condemnation is the deepest root that brings fear, stress, and all kinds of sickness. Condemnation literally kills you. The answer is the foundation of grace, and let us be known for our graciousness:

"Blessed is the man who trusts in the LORD, and whose hope is the LORD,

For he shall be like a tree planted by the waters, which spreads out its roots by the river, and will not fear when heat comes; but its leaf will be green and will not be anxious in the year of drought, nor will cease from yielding fruit" (Jeremiah 17:7–8 NKJV).

Jesus will cause you to be a picture of robust strength and vitality. The blessed man will not be anxious in the year of drought (or a share market crash).

Remember: The Old Covenant of law is all about you, but the New Covenant of grace is all about Jesus. Why did God choose Mount Zion and not Mount Sinai? Mount Zion represents grace, and Mount Sinai represented law.

James 2:10 (NKJV) says, "For whoever shall keep the whole law, and yet stumble in one point, he is guilty of all."

See the difference between the two covenants when it comes to our salvation?

Old Covenant:

"Keeping mercy for thousands, forgiving iniquity and transgression and sin, by no means clearing the guilty, visiting the iniquity of the fathers upon the children and the children's children to the third and fourth generation" (Exodus 34:7 NKJV).

New Covenant:

"For I will be merciful to their unrighteousness, and their sins and their lawless deeds I will remember no more" (Hebrews 8:12 NKJV).

The same God is speaking, so what happened? The cross happened. The law exposes sin; it cannot cleanse, cover, or remove sin.

The Bible declares the Old Covenant to be obsolete in Hebrews 8:13:

"Therefore let it be known to you, brethren, that through this Man is preached to you the forgiveness of sins;

and by Him everyone who believes is justified from all things from which you could not be justified by the law of Moses" (Acts 13:38–39 NKJV).

Under grace, if you do one thing right (and that is to believe on the Lord Jesus Christ), then you will be justified from all. Those trying to be justified by their law keeping still have an Old Covenant mentality, even if they profess to be in the New Covenant. They have reverted to the old system that was based on works and obedience, rather than trusting in the new system that is based on faith and believing. When you mix the Old Covenant of the law with the New Covenant of grace, you lose both, and the benefits are nullified.

"I know your works, that you are neither cold nor hot. I could wish you were cold or hot.

So then, because you are lukewarm, and neither cold nor hot, I will vomit you out of My mouth" (Revelation 3:15–16 NKJV).

Cold: Entirely under the law.

Hot: Entirely under grace.

The law would reveal your sinfulness and inability to keep it.

Grace gives you undeserved favour and an opportunity to repent.

Lukewarm: Robs you of your power.

The law makes everything of man's effort, while grace gives all the glory to God. The hearing of faith and the works of the law are totally opposite. When you get a revelation (unveiling of the truth), you will know in your heart (not your head) that grace will enable miracles to happen in your life.

Mark 5:34 (NKJV) says, "And He said to her, 'Daughter, your faith has made you well. Go in peace, and be healed of your affliction.'"

When she saw His grace, He (Jesus) turned around and saw her faith. Faith for any breakthrough or miracle in your life springs forth when you see His grace.

Note: You do not put your faith in your faith; you put it in God's grace and love, for faith works by love.

Ephesians 3:20 (NKJV) says, "Now to Him who is able to do exceedingly abundantly above all that we ask or think, according to the power that works in us."

Receive an abundance of grace, a gift of righteousness, and start reigning in life over sin, sickness, financial lack, and the curse of the law through the one, Christ Jesus. The New Covenant is based entirely on His unmerited favour. Our part is to have faith in Jesus to enjoy the New Covenant blessing through His finished work.

If you are trying to obey the Old Covenant and also the New Covenant, you are being double-minded, and the Bible says a double-minded man is unstable in all his ways. In the New Covenant, you do not have to depend on favouritism to keep opportunities open for yourself, when you have God's unmerited favour. Luke 5:4–7 shows their reward for obedience was a net-breaking, boat-sinking load of fish.

God's presence is with you, to direct you, guide you, and lead you into becoming more like Christ. His Grace and His ability in you will make you a success in every endeavour you undertake.

Proverbs 3:6 (NKJV) says, "In all your ways acknowledge Him, and He shall direct your paths."

Grace enables you to have success beyond your natural abilities and in spite of any negative environment because the Lord is with you. Remember: Feelings are not based on truth; God's word is truth.

Grace (divine empowerment of God in your life) will enable you to accomplish things way above your natural talents. Anyone can count the seeds of an apple, but only God can count the apples in a seed. God is in the multiplying business. He can take what little you have and bless it. The five loaves and two fish, the young boy's lunch, fed over twelve thousand people, with twelve baskets of food left over.

We are His precious children; He wants us to give to Him out of love and desire, not out of obligation or duty. When our "want tos" towards God fade and shift into "ought tos," the joy is drained away. The law kills; it kills worship and joy. It kills spontaneity and credulity; it kills freedom. It kills relationships and families. It even kills churches. The law was referred to as the ministry of death in 2 Corinthians 3:7–8. The Old Covenant is headed by Adam; the New Covenant is headed by Christ.

Gospel Patrons

The following great people of faith are well known, but few Christians know the people who supported them financially. They all gave generously, as love and grace filled their hearts to see the kingdom of God preached:

- Humphrey Monmouth supported William Tyndale in the 1500s.
- Three gracious women (Mary, Jenna, and Susanna) provided for the disciples.
- Priscilla and Aquila supported Paul.
- Lady Huntingdale supported George Whitfield.
- John Thornton supported John Newton.

In conclusion, walking in divine grace will prevent psychology being exalted above discernment, theology above revelation, programs above the leading of the Holy Spirit, reasoning above the walk of faith, and laws above love.

Now that we know what grace is and how it works, let's look at the global financial system and how we can take advantage of it at a personal level.

Hosea 4:6 (NKJV) says, "My people are destroyed for lack of knowledge."

Let's not be taken by surprise and apply all the legitimate means at our disposal to get through this coming financial Armageddon, should almighty God delay the second coming of Jesus longer than we thought. Live as if He is coming back tomorrow, and plan as if you will make it to retirement.

PART 3

The Global Financial System

Here are some sobering facts as of December, 2016. We are in unchartered waters after nearly twenty years of madcap money printing by the US Federal Reserve and other central banks. Everything has been widely inflated: shares, banks, real estate, and also the entire real economy, as measured by global gross domestic product (GDP). The world's central banks are finally out of dry powder. They no longer have the means to inflate the global credit and financial bubble. We are hurtling into a prolonged worldwide deflation. The writing is on the wall; we see the plunge in oil, iron, copper, and other commodity prices.

The central banks cannot generate more credit, no matter how hard they try because most of the world has reached peak debt. Most of us, including companies and governments, are stuck with such monumental debt, they cannot service any additional debt, no matter what the interest rate (even zero or below). Japan is a basket case: a prime example that massive money printing is not working. Public and private debt is 450 percent of GDP. Now despite years of zero interest rates, the Bank of Japan credit stopped growing long ago. Japan is now in its fifth recession in seven years.

Jeremiah said in 17:9 (NKJV) "The heart is deceitful above all things and desperately wicked; who can know it?" The heart of the problem is the problem of the human heart. Mankind has a sinful nature and consequently has a flawed nature. The scriptures further state in Proverbs 16:25 (NKJV) "There is a way that seems right to a man, but its end is the way of death."

How did we ever get to this intractable point? Let's start with the world's largest economy and see who is really running the United States government and its economy. Our modern economy was conceived on Jekyll Island, Georgia, by six men, who represented one-quarter of the entire wealth of the world: Nelson W. Aldrich (the father-in-law to John D. Rockefeller), Abraham Piatt Andrew (assistant secretary of the US Treasury), Frank A. Vanderlip (president of National City Bank of New York), Henry P. Davison (senior partner of J.P. Morgan), Benjamin Strong (head of J.P. Morgan's Bankers Trust), and Paul Warburg (of the Rothschild banking dynasty. Rockefeller, Rothschild, Warburg, and Morgan secretly met in 1910 and made an eight hundred-mile trip from New York to Atlanta to Savannah to Brunswick, Georgia. They had a clandestine meeting and sent the current hotel staff on a two-week holiday, replacing them with their own hotel staff who had to sign a secrecy agreement that they would not disclose any information regarding the meeting. At the meeting, they decided on how to control the world's money supply and came up with a Government sounding name called the "Federal Reserve", which is really a cabal of incredibly wealthy bankers who have private ownership of the capital that is put into the Federal Reserve supply. They fought the case at Congress who eventually acquiesced to the printing of money and further put in one Governor which later grew to twelve Federal Reserve (Central Banks) each with its own Governor. It was meant to be a bank of last resort if investment banks went bust, but these billionaires controlled and orchestrated booms and busts. In 1914, the Federal Reserve Act became law.

A cartel is a group of independent businesses which join together to co-ordinate the production, pricing, or marketing of their members. The goal of a cartel is to maximise profits by minimising competition between members and make it difficult for new competitors to enter the field.

In 1913, 716 non-national banks held 57 percent of the country's deposits. The balance between debt and savings was the result of a limited money supply, backed by gold. Banks had loaned out three hundred times more than the deposit amount, but as long as depositors didn't request their money all at once, no one was the wiser. Banks loaned up to 99 percent of reserves, which were failing because of currency drains.

Warburg was the mastermind of the Federal Reserve System. The Federal Reserve has not caused stability; instead, it led to the crash of 1921; the Great Depression (1929 to 1939); the recessions of 1953, 1959, 1969, and 1981; the stock market crash in 1987; and the global financial crash in 2007.

By 1990, inflation was so high that $10,000 could only buy what $1,000 did in 1914. Interest on the national debt is consuming 50 percent of the nation's personal income tax. The Federal Reserve is really a cartel with a government façade. The Federal Reserve is a legal private monopoly of the money supply, operated for the benefit of the few under the guise of protecting and promoting the public interest.

Note: Warburg and the others obtained a franchise to create money out of nothing, took control of all the reserves of all the banks, and left the taxpayer to pick up the cartel's inevitable losses.

The banks know that their huge loans to foreign governments ($100 billion) will not be paid out but just rolled over and so incur more interest. Rolling over the loan is a great way for the bank to get perpetual interest. Borrowing money constantly means even the interest can't be paid, so the bank lends more money to pay the ever-increasing interest; like a dog chasing its tail, it will never catch up, and so the loans will never be paid off. Borrowers finally reach peak debt and are unable to pay, and so after suffering threatening innuendos, they compromise and borrow more money and still have to pay for purchases. As a result, the bank has a greater asset, charges higher interest on the loan, and receives larger profits; what an exciting game!

When the interest is more than a country's tax base or company's entire corporate earnings, it becomes necessary to reschedule and lower the interest rate and extend the time to pay. This eases the burden and postpones the day of reckoning. On the day of reckoning, the bank and the borrower approach the government for a bail-out. The impoverished country is desperate and is then put on an austerity program, which puts them in a position to obtain a new loan, and so the cycle starts all over again. The dog never stops chasing its tail.

The Federal Deposit Insurance Corporation (FDIC) covers all banks, both good and bad, and encourages profligacy (reckless lending).

Valuating private insurance: good banks, low premiums.

Risky banks, high premiums.

Insolvent banks, no premiums.

Summary

- All money in the banking system has been created out of nothing.
- Large bad debts are rolled over and increased in size.
- Get the government to guarantee the loan.

- Use the Federal Deposit Insurance Corporation to pay off the loan.
- When FDIC funds run out, balance is paid by Federal Reserve System.
- Final cost of the bailout therefore is passed on to the public in the form of a hidden tax called inflation.

Major Banks that were bailed out in the 2008 financial crisis

- Bank of America $45 billion
- Citi Group $45 billion
- JP Morgan Chase $25 billion
- Wells Fargo $25 billion
- GMAC (now Ally Financial) $16.29 billion
- Goldman Sachs $10 billion
- Morgan Stanley $10 billion

And the two Government sponsored enterprises received the following -

- Fannie Mae $116.149 billion
- Freddie Mac $71.336 billion

And the large insurance company -

- AIG $67.835 billion

Savings and Loans Scandal

- Great distortion of supply and demand by subsidised home mortgages.
- Flood of cheap money; home prices rose artificially.
- Bust, with many savings and loans becoming insolvent.

- Accounting gimmicks show insolvent banks as solvent.
- Failed savings and loans continued to lose billions of dollars each month.
- Trillion-dollar bailout had to come from taxes and inflation.

World Bank Loans and Massive Failures

- In India, the World Bank funded the construction of a dam that displaced two million people, flooded three hundred square miles, and wiped out eighty-one thousand acres of forest.
- Tanzania took out a $3 billion loan; in 1986, it was an exporter of food and now imports food.
- Argentina had one of the highest standards of living to 1989 and reached an all-time high of 20,262% in March of 1990.
- Brazil in 1990 had inflation rate of 5,000 percent. Since 1960, prices have risen 164,000 times their original level.

Summary of World Bank Involvement

- The World Bank and the International Monetary Fund (IMF) was created at Bretton Woods, New Hampshire, in 1944.
- Creating money out of nothing (as done by Federal Reserve Bank) and lending it is a Socialist enterprise.
- The World Bank created massive inflation and debt to nations.
- "Monetise" is banker language for creating money out of nothing, for the purpose of lending to foreign governments, to make money out of government debt.

The Bolshevik revolution was actually financed by wealthy financiers in London and New York.

Building the New World Order

- The main money goes from the Federal Reserve through the IMF and World Bank.
- More money is lent to defaulting loans, so that the interest payments can continue going to the banks.
- The objective is to give the IMF/World Bank the power to issue a world fiat currency, to build a world government.
- The IMF/World Bank directs the massive transfer of wealth from the industrialised nations to the less-developed nations. This ongoing process eventually drains the economies to a point where they will also need assistance. No longer capable of independent action, they will accept the loss of sovereignty in return for international aid.
- The true goal of the transfer of wealth disguised as loans is to get control over the leaders of the less-developed countries.
- These despots become like gold-plated cogs in the giant machinery of world government; they don't care what ideology it is: capitalist, communist, socialist, fascist, as long as the money keeps coming in.
- China and the former Soviet bloc are the latest recipient countries; they are already in arrears in payment.

Money: How It Really Works

Monopolies control prices and make the average person pay more than they ought to. When the quantity of money expands without a corresponding increase in goods, the effect is a reduction in the purchasing power of each monetary unit.

In 1913, the average wage per annum in the United States was $633, which is equal to 30.6 ounces of gold (at $20.67 per ounce).

In 1990, the average wage per annum in the United States was $20,468, which is equal to 52.09 ounces of gold (at $386.90 per ounce).

In 2014, the average wage per annum in the United States was $57,000, which is equal to 47.5 ounces of gold (at $1,200 per ounce).

In the absence of the gold standard, there is no way to prevent savings from eroding through inflation.

The Byzantine Empire traded gold coins that were made to such a high standard that they never chipped or devalued, and they flourished for eight hundred years. In those rare instances where man has refrained from manipulating the money supply and has allowed it to be determined by free market production of the gold supply, there has been prosperity and tranquillity.

Fiat money is paper money that has not been backed up by gold. In 1750 in Connecticut, prices rose by 800 percent, in Carolina by 900 percent, and in Massachusetts by 1000 percent.

Note: Booms and busts were direct manifestations of the expansion and contraction of the fiat money.

In 1775, the Continental Army had $12 million of its own currency in circulation. In 1779, it had $425 million in circulation (that is 3,500 percent inflation). A pair of shoes cost $5,000 and a suit of clothes $1,000,000; that is where the saying "Not worth a continental" came from. Legal tender status was not conferred upon the bank's money until 1833. The first central bank, the Bank of England, was created in 1694 in London.

Note: The gold reserve put a brake on the amount of money that can be created.

Summary

Banks began in Europe in the fourteenth century. They issued honest paper receipts backed up by gold and silver coins. In time, they became dishonest and issued more loans than were backed up by coins, so it became fractional reserve banking. There was an unbroken record of booms and busts, inflation, and bank failures.

The Bank of England formed in 1694 was the first central bank. The politicians received spendable money created out of nothing by the bankers, without having to raise taxes. Bankers received a commission on transactions, which they called interest.

Note: If the money we are borrowing was earned by someone's labour and talent, they would be fully entitled to receive interest on it. But what are we to think of money that is created by the mere click of a computer key? The Federal Reserve has a legal right to issue credit: money created out of nothing.

The definition of "monetise" is to convert into money any amount of government debt.

The Federal Reserve is an association of large commercial banks that have been granted special privileges. It is a cartel, protected by federal law; a cartel is an association of independent enterprises to monopolise production and distribution of a product or service. By controlling the supply of money through a central bank, you can control the political system of a country.

The bottom line is, if you can control a nation's money, you don't care which party gets in. The Rothschild dynasty began in Frankfurt, Germany, in the middle of the eighteenth century; their five sons promoted fractional reserve banking. The Rothschild dynasty financed Cecil Rhodes, who established a monopoly of the diamond fields of South Africa. Lord Alfred Milner spent twenty-one million roubles to finance the Russian revolution.

Insider Trading

Here is the classic of all classics of insider trading, perpetrated by Nathan Rothschild. At midnight on June 18, 1815, Rothschild's agent consigned his finest horse to speed back from Port Ostend of the English Channel, to report the outcome of the Duke of Wellington's war. Twelve hours before the official notification of the government, Rothschild knew that the Duke of Wellington had won the Battle of Waterloo. He went to the stock exchange and gave orders to sell all his bonds. News spread like wildfire that Wellington must have lost the war. The price of the government bonds tumbled. Near the closing time, he reversed the order to buy all government bonds at the fire sale prices. The next day, news came officially that the Duke of Wellington had actually won, and the bonds soared. He made millions in one single day, an astronomical amount in today's value.

The Council for Foreign Relations is a front for the J.P. Morgan dynasty. Almost all of the members of the Council for Foreign Relations are in key positions in government; it was later backed by the Rockefellers. After the Russian revolution, agents of the Council for Foreign Relations, backed by J.P. Morgan, cashed in on his close friendship with Trotsky and Lenin and obtained profitable business concessions from the new government.

Morgan used the Red Cross as a front to send money that was then forwarded on to all factions of the revolutionary movement, to be sure of gaining influence with whoever was winning the war. The bottom line is that ideology can sway revolutionary operators like Kerensky, Lenin, and Trotsky, but not financiers. To justify the coming new world government, there must be a crisis created using frightful weapons. So in reality, the financiers are not pro-communist; they are working to bring Russia and America into a world government.

The progression of the monetary system is as follows:

- On July 6, 1785, Congress unanimously voted to adopt the Spanish dollar as the official monetary unit of the United States.
- In 1792, the Coinage Act was passed; the punishment for debasing the nation's monetary system was the death penalty. The bottom line is, if this was applied today, the Federal Reserve, the House of Representatives, the Senate, the Treasury Department, and the president would all face the death penalty. Amazingly, by 1802, there was no federal deficit, no paper money, and no fiat money.

Summary

- The Constitution prohibits state and federal governments from issuing fiat money.
- The adopted Spanish dollar had to contain 371 grains of pure silver.
- 1793–1808 was a period of sound money and great economic prosperity.

Key point: Unlike paper money, gold represented real value and true worth.

Why do the elite create busts to reap the profits of foreclosed homes, farms, and businesses? The ultra-rich have tremendous influence on our educational system; for example, the University of Chicago was endowed by John D. Rockefeller with nearly $50 million. Directors of banks wore many caps; Cleveland H. Dodge and Cyrus McCormack, who were directors of Rockefeller's National City Bank, were also trustees of Princeton University.

There are only four ways to increase bank reserves:

- attract more deposits
- use some of the bank's deposits
- sell shares
- borrow money from the Federal Reserve

Each dollar of new reserves from the Federal Reserve can be used to lend out nine more dollars; that is called fractional reserve banking today.

Most people do not know what the Federal Reserve is. The Fed is an association of large commercial banks, which have been granted special privileges by Congress; it is a cartel protected by federal law.

Now, we are going to look at key points about the one world government and one world financial system. A new currency has been proposed called the "amero," which will unite Canada, the United States, and Mexico as a united bloc. The US currency is being nationalised, which is a polite word for socialism.

Note: State-controlled capitalism is an old-fashioned word for socialism. The concepts of globalisation and nationalisation were the antithesis of what America's founding fathers stood for. Many people do not know that on the back of the US dollar bill is a pyramid with words *"Novus Ordo Seclorum,"* which means "new order of the ages" or "new world order." The truth of the matter is America is no longer run by we the people; it is run by a shadow government that pulls the strings of our elected officials, courts, the economy, and president. The world government to come, is what the ancient Hebrew prophet Daniel referred to as the fourth beast (Daniel chapter 9). The sad truth is, America's rejection of God and His laws, that is, America's promotion of idolatry and immorality, plus the US and the EU currently dividing the land of Israel, are contributing to the global financial crisis. God has a foreign policy; it is mentioned in Genesis

12:1–3 (NKJV): "I will bless those who bless you and I'll curse those who curse you."

American manufacturing cannot compete against China because in 2005, the labour rate in China was seventy-nine cents per hour, while in America, it was $16.30 per hour. In 2014, the rate in China was $4.08 per hour, and in America, it was $22.30 per hour. Many businessmen thought, '*Why bother to start a new small business when you can just borrow from the Federal Reserve and buy your own shares?*'

Now let's look at US government spending: In 1916, the US government took in $783 million and spent $734 million. In 1919, the US government took in $5.1 billion and spent $18.5 billion. In 1919, taxes provided just 28 percent, and the rest was borrowed. The amazing thing is the Federal Reserve buys up the debt of its own government. Wage earners should receive interest income instead of paying an income tax. The Federal Reserve should not lend the US Treasury newly printed money. In 1917, US debt was $19.2 billion. Amazingly, by 2014, it was $17.5 trillion, and by 2017, it was $19.9 trillion.

Materialism has really caught on in America with the increased production of goods; for example, in 1920, only nineteen Americans per thousand had motor cars. In 2016, most families are paying off one or two cars.

The Great Depression (1929–1939) lasted almost ten years, and many families never really recovered from it. There is also a great improvement in life span; we are simply living longer, and the government has to find ways to fund the ageing population. In 1920, the average life expectancy was 56.4 years, and in 2010, it was 78.7 years. The average wage in 1920 was $1,342 per annum, and in 2010, it was $39,959. The federal government debt in 1920 was $25.9 billion, and in 2010 it was $9 trillion. It jumped to $18 trillion in 2015. In part 4 of this book, you will see that you have to start planning now; you will not be able to rely on the age pension in any of the world's 157 countries.

Here is an example of what inflation does: In 1919, a silk shirt cost $16; the same silk shirt in 2015 would be $202. So more money in pursuit of the same volume of goods points to higher prices, printing money is not the answer. In 1923, Germany's exchange rate was 1.2 trillion marks to the US dollar, and in 2008, Zimbabwe had to print 100 trillion dollar notes. Unfortunately, we are deemed to repeat the past because we have not learned from it.

The best way to think of quantitative easing (fiat money) is sub-prime lending on a global scale. The truth of the matter is, $100 trillion of liquid wealth is overseen by mutual funds, hedge funds, insurance companies, sovereign wealth funds, and pension funds; they own virtually no gold.

Here are some examples of a drastic drop of purchasing power by some countries. In 1994, the Mexican peso dropped 39 percent in forty-two days. In 1997, Thailand's currency, the baht, lost 23 percent in twenty-five days and then 41 percent in the following six months. Brazil (in 1996), Russia (in 1998), Argentina (in 2001), South Korea (in 2007), and Iceland (in 2008) all suffered huge losses. Inflation has forced 44 million Americans to rely on food stamps. Since 1913, the American dollar has lost 95 percent of its value; a cup of coffee was only fifteen cents and now it is $3.50. The joke about Iceland is, "Why couldn't people get out their money? Because their assets were frozen."

Here are some sobering facts about America: True unemployment, counting underemployment, is 25 percent. 50 percent of US households receive some form of government benefits; 60 percent of Americans have less than $25,000 in total savings, and the US government pumps $85 billion per month ($1 trillion per year) with quantitative easing. The federal government debt is now $19.9 trillion.

Remuneration for CEOs is way out of whack; for example, thirty years ago, senior executive incomes was forty times the average weekly earnings; in 2014, it was 880 times. The extreme money belonged to hedge fund managers. Amazingly, they earned President Obama's annual salary of $500,000 in two and a half hours (that is $200,000 per hour or $8 million per week).

The global financial crisis showed there was no moral accountability; for example, when there were record profits, the bankers took the credit, claiming it was due to their efforts. When there were record losses, they were the results of forces beyond their control.

The truth about the US Federal Reserve is, these are privately owned banks, but they act as a financial arm of the government. The Federal Reserve issues IOU's to the Treasury so it does not have to sell its bonds at a loss. In 2007–2009, the Fed should have closed insolvent banks and not bailed them out. Recently, President Obama stated that America has the largest economy in the world. He forgot to say it has the largest government debt in the world.

Dishonesty Pays a Heavy Price

Dishonesty costs the American public nearly 10 percent of the price of goods displayed in retail stores, due to the cost of insurance against theft. Perjury defrauds the US Internal Revenue Service out of billions of dollars each year, through dishonest tax returns. Complete honesty in this area would go a long way to address the $19.4 trillion deficit.

Poverty Elevation

Here are some interesting but disturbing facts about poverty:

- In 2015, one billion people lived on $1 per day, at the same time the average American lived on $148 per day and the average Australian lived on $176 per day.
- 40 percent (2.8 billion) inhabitants struggle just to eat every day.
- 2.5 million Australians are living in poverty today.

Four Categories of Poverty

- poverty of spiritual intimacy (that is, denying God's existence)
- poverty of stewardship (that is, loss of sense of poverty)
- poverty of community (that is, self-centredness and abuse of others)
- poverty of being (that is, low self-esteem)

Poverty is a result of broken relationships, where there is no harmony or enjoyment. Poverty is the absence of peace and all its meanings.

Poverty requires the ministry of reconciliation, moving people closer to glorifying God by living in right relationship with God, with self, with others, and with creation. Healthy relationships require transformed hearts, not just transformed brains. The New Testament has a lot to say about caring for the poor, and this should be a vital concern for the church.

Scripture references include Matthew 25:31–46, Acts 6:1–7, Galatians 2:1–10 and 6:10, and James 1:27.

How useless it would have been if Jesus had only used words and not deeds to declare His kingdom (Luke 18:35–43).

This sin-cursed earth has created poverty; sin entered our nature, so our character is flawed. Subsequently, it is easier to blame people's faults because they are more obvious to see than the fallen systems in which we live. The bottom line is, we must introduce materially poor people to the only One who can truly reconcile the broken relationships that underline their material poverty.

The government knows that a crisis is the best opportunity to get people to surrender their freedom, for the promise of security. America, for example, has a $19.9 trillion federal government debt, state government debt of $1.3 trillion, and local government debt of $1.8 trillion. In 2011, the US government spent $3.6 trillion but received only $2.3 trillion. The $1.3 trillion shortfall was borrowed. The sad fact is Americans are labouring under $13 trillion in mortgage debt.

The difference between China and America, for example, is that China imports mainly coal and iron ore to make steel, while America imports mainly electronics, toys, and sporting goods for personal consumption. The US government is using borrowed money to pay out its debt obligations; for example, it owes $1.2 trillion (plus interest) to China in Treasury bonds. Amazingly, in 1980, the United States was the world's largest creditor nation; by 2014, it was the largest debtor nation. In 1913, the Federal Reserve was created to be the bank of last resort, not to prop up government spending with money made out of thin air. In reality, the US government has its own magic piggy bank: The Federal Reserve.

The only real money is gold and not fiat money (printed money not backed up by gold); look at the consistent value of gold: In 1779, $100 of gold was worth $2,600 Continental notes. By 1781, it was worth $16,800 Continental notes, and in 1783, the Continental was worthless.

Now the classic case of hyperinflation was the Weimar government in Germany. For example, in 1919, there were twelve marks to the US dollar. In 1921, there were fifty-seven marks to the US dollar. In October 1923, there were 170 billion marks to the US dollar, and a mere two months later (December 1923), there were one trillion marks to the US dollar.

In 1971, President Nixon knew that the US government could no longer redeem money with gold and suspended the conversion of the dollar into gold; the public had to accept fiat money. The American governments of the past have never learned the lesson about inflation; as the saying goes, 'It is insane to do the same thing over and over again and expect to get a different result.'

Quantitative easing is really just printing money; banks increase the quantity of money and reduce interest rates. When you hear economists or reserve bank officials using the phrase "debt monetisation," it is really turning debt into circulating currency. Quantitative easing is like giving a heroin addict a bigger shot of heroin; it only alleviates withdrawal symptoms for a while. Amazingly, the total of US government commitments is a staggering $95 trillion, yet its gross domestic product is only $18 trillion. So in reality, the debt is $1.1 million per family of four Americans. If we look at the GDP of the world, it is $69 trillion, but the combined total of derivatives (that is, taking bets on interest rates) and currency movements is a staggering $690 trillion. The sad fact is that in 1999, Congress overturned the Glass-Steagall Act of 1935; that meant that commercial banks could now take risks like investment banks. For two centuries, there was monetary stability up until 1971 because the classical gold standard enabled the national currency to hold its value.

The cost of maintaining military spending is a huge drain on any economy, but America spends most of its GDP on its military. For example, the United States spends $682 billion (or 4.4 percent of GDP). China spends $166 billion (or 2 percent of GDP), Russia spends $91 billion (or 4.4 percent of GDP), and the United Kingdom spends $61 billion (or 2.5 percent of GDP). When gold spikes, it is a sign that global capital is losing its faith in fiat currency. James Rickards wrote a book in 2016 called *The New Case for Gold*; his research has shown that gold is about to spike.

Most people do not know that the US Federal Reserve is not actually a branch of the government, but instead a private consortium of major banks with twelve regional branches, each run by a governor and by the president. The golden rule is "Don't put all your eggs in the one basket." And for those who invested only in real estate, this will be brought home. In 2006, the US housing market peaked and then subsequently fell by 34 percent, leading to a record number of foreclosures and financial ruin of countless American families.

In the coming decade, as the dollar suffers one of the greatest meltdowns in monetary history, gold will reclaim its place at the centre of the global financial system. Another example of the devastating effects of inflation was in Rome; in AD 301, one pound of gold was worth 50,000 denari; in 307, it was worth 100,000 denari; in 324, it was worth 300,000 denary; in 350, it was worth 2 billion denary; in 410, the denary was worthless, and Rome fell to the Visigoths (barbarians).

Bureaucracy is a killer; in the Federal Reserve regulations, there were 4,000 pages in 1936, 12,000 pages in 1950, 40,000 pages in 1980, and 70,000 pages in 2007.

Economists have estimated that the US cost of government (that is, federal, state, and local) is $3 trillion. In 1690, the first paper currency was issued by the Bank of England; in 1699, King William III appointed Sir Isaac Newton to be master of the mint; this brilliant man knew that money was only a substitute. It had to be linked to gold, and so he linked gold to bank-issued currency, and that became known as the classical gold standard, causing great stability in the monetary system.

In the United States in 1860, there were eight thousand privately owned banks circulating dozens of private currencies; it was an absolute disaster, so one year later, in 1861, during the Civil War, Abraham Lincoln brought in a new currency called "the greenback." To discourage state-owned chartered banks, a 10 percent tax was imposed in 1863; this greatly curtailed currency printing. Businesses favoured the newly formed national banks, using only the greenback. From 1870 to 1914, economic stability was achieved because currency had to be backed up by gold. This consequently limited the amount of money the government could print.

South Korea's Amazing Economic Growth

Four million people died in the Korean War (1950–1953); this devastated their economy. In 1938, Samsung exported only fish and vegetables; in 1974, it entered the semi-conductor business. In 1961, the average annual income in South Korea was $82. In 1975, the average South Korean worked fifty-three hours per week. The same year, Hong Kong's per capita income was 3.5 times that of South Korea. In 1996, South Korea joined the Organisation for Economic Cooperation and Development (OECD). In 1963, the average lifespan in South Korea was just fifty-three years. In 2014, the average life span was seventy-seven years. In 1963, baby deaths were seventy-eight per thousand; in 2014, baby deaths were five per thousand.

Neoliberal economics achieved low inflation, small government, private enterprise, free trade, and friendliness towards foreign investment. Free trade in reality reduces freedom of choice for poor countries imposed by the IMF and the World Bank. The fall of communism in 1989 was a result of neoliberalism economics.

Disturbing US Facts

- The four biggest banks are now 30 percent larger than in 2007.
- The five largest banks hold more than half of the total banking assets in the United States.
- US debt has blown out to $19.9 trillion in 2017.
- Derivatives have been called "financial weapons of mass destruction." The market is now $7 hundred trillion, ten times bigger than the entire world economy.

- The United States will lose its coveted status as the world's reserve currency.
- In 2015, most US jobs being created were too low paying and too insecure to support the purchase of a home. Corporate executives find it more profitable to fund stock buybacks, or buy competitive companies and sack workers, than to invest in their work force.

Poor Economics

- 936 million people, 13 percent of the world's population, struggle on $1 per day.
- Every year, nine million children die before their fifth birthday.
- In twenty-five countries, people are not expected to live more than fifty-five years.
- 25 percent of the world's population don't have access to safe drinking water.
- 42 percent of the world's population live without a toilet at home.
- Every year of extra schooling, on an average, increases their income by 8 percent.

The bottom line for the poor is, they lack critical information, and they bear responsibility for too many aspects of their lives; they also get negative interest rates and pay exorbitant rates on their loans.

Israel's Financial Miracle

Since 1948, Israel's population has grown tenfold, the arable land threefold, agricultural output sixteenfold, and industrial output fiftyfold; water usage has dropped an astounding 10 percent. This nation has clearly been blessed by God.

Global Economic Malaise

- Licensing laws are killing small businesses. Hundreds of state regulations deter entrepreneurs from starting new businesses.
- Antidiscrimination laws actually incentivise discrimination.
- Banks in the United States took huge risks, knowing they were going to be bailed out.
- The Federal Reserve bailed out the Federal Deposit Insurance Corporation, Fanny Mae, Bear Stearns, AIG, and Troubled Asset Relief Program.
- In the United States, both political parties employ the Keynesian economic principles "spend your way to prosperity."
- A truly sad fact is, Americans have aborted approximately fifty million babies since 1970, costing the American economy $35 trillion in lost productivity.
- Greece and Spain both had 27 percent unemployment in 2014.

One World Government and One World Financial System

International banking empires of J.P. Morgan, Eugene Myer, Lazard Freres, M.M. Warburg, and the Rothschild brothers really control America. When you look at Russia, China, North Vietnam, Cuba, and Venezuela, you see masses of poor people, almost no middle class, and a very, very wealthy elite class that controls everything. Paul Warburg helped America and England to finance WWI, and his brother, Max Warburg, lent Germany billions of dollars to finance the war. Dr Adam Weishaupt founded the Illuminati in 1776; followed a Luciferian doctrine and called for the abolition of -

- sovereign nationalistic governments,
- private property,
- inheritance rights,
- patriotism,

- traditional family moral codes and sexual prohibition laws,
- religious disciplines based on faith, and
- global taxation.

International criminal court was to replace US courts, and the continent of North America (Canada, Mexico, and the United State) was to be unified under a new currency called the "amero."

Australian Economy

Australian trading banks used a facility offered by the reserve bank known as a "lender of last resort." This was removed during the 1980s. The global financial crisis precipitated a new scheme called the financial claim scheme, which covered all authorised deposit institutions in Australia. This includes all banks, building societies, and credit unions. Depositors are compensated up to $250,000 per account per financial institution. Fractional reserve banking is where trading banks lend out nine times what their capital reserves are. The Australian government has reined this in by requiring greater capital resources, from 11 cents in the dollar to 25 cents in the dollar; that means they can only loan out four times their capital reserves as loans.

The Australian banking system has a monopoly called the big four; they are Commonwealth, National Bank, West Pac, and ANZ. The Reserve Bank of Australia killed off the 2009 potential recovery by raising interest rates. It beggars belief that the RBA and Australian Prudential Regulatory Authority don't let the law of supply and demand set property prices.

Investment Prosperity

In Australia, millionaires account for more than one-third of the assets in property, compared to 20 percent globally. Where do millionaires put their money? Globally, 26.8 percent invest in the share market, 25.6 percent in cash, 17.6 percent in real estate, 16.9 percent in fixed income, and 13 percent in alternatives. In Asia Pacific, 22.8 percent is in the share market, 23.1 percent in cash, 23.1 percent in real estate, 18.7 percent in fixed income, and 14 percent in alternatives. In Australia, 22 percent is in the share market, 22 percent in cash, 35 percent in real estate, 11 percent in fixed income, and 10 percent in alternatives. But investing in knowledge still brings the most wealth.

We as a world economy have gone past the point of no return; past-peak debt is now irreversible. Some financial experts estimate the world's debt exceeds $1.5 quadrillion; this includes public and private unfunded liabilities and outstanding derivatives (derivatives are financial instruments whose value is derived from the price of another financial asset; e.g., bonds made up from different levels of mortgages and repackaged into mortgage-backed bonds. Derivatives are typically used for hedging and speculative purposes. They are not regulated by the Securities and Exchange Commission (SEC).

Many world leaders believe the creation of a new global financial system will help prevent future economic crises. Incredibly, the Bible predicted nearly two thousand years ago, that a global dictator would take control of the world economy; it also forecast a cashless society. This prediction is contained in Revelation 13:16–18. When Lucifer, the "serpent of old," instigated the fall of man, he became temporary "god of this world." As such, Lucifer created economic, government, and religious systems based upon satanic ideas; this was called the Babylonian or world system:

"With your wisdom and your understanding you have gained riches for yourself, and gathered gold and silver into your treasuries" (Ezekiel 28:4 NKJV).

The international banking system was set up in the late eighteenth century by the barbarian Illuminati. The very wealthiest people in the world are fully aware of this, and that is why a select few, who actually control the world's wealth, belong to organisations such as Skull and Bones, Bohemian Grove, and the Bilderberg Group. The elite understand that ultimately the economy is connected to a Luciferian spiritual economic system.

The highest levels of government finance, culture, science, and politics, the elite, are busy constructing a global economic order that will culminate in what is described in Revelation as the mark of the beast system. We can see this with the development of biometrics, radio frequency identification (RFID) chips, electronic tattoos, electronic payments, and similar technologies. Prophesy scholars say that the mark of the beast system is now possible for the first time in history.

Just before the end of World War II, officials from forty-four nations gathered together to Bretton Woods, New Hampshire, to lay the groundwork for a new international economic system. This meeting would bring about the transformation of a global and financial economic order.

In his book *The Shemitah*, Johnathan Cahn links the shemitah to one of the most shocking events in American history: the September 11, 2001, terrorist attacks. As the twenty-first century began, the tower that represented our eminence of economic dominance fell and crashed on 9/11. America has been defiant just as Israel was and quoted the scripture from Isaiah 9:10 "The bricks have fallen but we will rebuild with human stones." America needs to come to a place of repentance and humble themselves to come under God's protection and needs to learn from the history of the past, the devastation that comes out of rebellion.

The underlying problem of the financial meltdown in 2007 was greed. Jeremiah the prophet said, "The heart of man is desperately wicked above all things." The result of sin from our first ancestors, Adam and Eve, has resulted in a flawed nature. Great intelligence does not mean great moral values; in fact, it can get you into greater trouble. Wall Street greed and government complicity, through the Fanny Mae and Freddie Mac agencies, guaranteed increasingly risky types of loans, combined with Wall Street derivatives, would eventually destroy the whole financial system, costing the US taxpayer tens of billions in losses. Let's look in more detail at the paper trail that led to the greatest economic meltdown since the 1929 Great Depression.

In the 1980s, inflation disappeared, the economy began growing, and lower interest rates caused a massive rally in the bond market. Now baby boomers, seeing these lower interest rates, decided to take out mortgages, and the market exploded. Wall Street financial engineers came up with the idea of repackaging all the mortgages into bonds and selling them off to investors. The new bond was called a collateralised mortgage obligation (CMO). The CMO was defined as a type of mortgage-backed security that is supported by a wide pool of mortgage loans. A CMO is typically divided into several classes that offer various cash flows to the bondholders. The first CMO hit the market in 1983.

In the United States, the twelve Federal Reserve Banks could not really control the use of derivatives because most of these bonds were hidden off the balance sheets; because the products were so new, no regulatory authority could supervise them. It was like the Wild West; there was not enough law enforcement in the boom towns.

The problem with these mortgage-backed bonds is, if there is a sharp decline in interest rates, homeowners rush to refinance their loans (good for homeowners but bad for mortgage bondholders because the bonds reset to the new low interest rate).

There were many unfortunate casualties of the 1994 bond market crash; Orange County, California, went bankrupt because it used public money to buy derivatives, and of course, Wall Street bond traders suffered as well.

Fanny Mae and Freddie Mac, two government-sponsored enterprises (GSEs), were using billions of dollars in debt each year, backed by an implied guarantee of payment by the federal government in case of defaults. The congressional mandate of promoting homeownership was now going beyond the original mandate of middle class ownership, and they were starting to offer home loans to people who could least afford it.

This was a huge disaster waiting to happen.

These below-par lending programs came to be known as sub-prime mortgages. Their goal was to increase homeownership to 70 percent; this was supported by New York's governor, Mario Cuomo. What fuelled this was the 1992 Federal Reserve Bank of Boston's statement that people were being denied mortgages purely on their race and income level, even if they had the means to repay them. When Cuomo became Housing and Urban Development secretary, he increased the amount from 42 to 50 percent that the government-sponsored enterprises had to set aside for low to moderate-income borrowers. The government was marching inexorably towards the coming economic meltdown.

The banks knew that they could sell off the loans to Wall Street banks, which would repackage them as mortgage-backed securities. So the lending criteria was lowered even further to include people with little or no credit history, some who could not document their incomes, and many others did not even have a regular job. These derivatives have been called a "monstrous global electronic Ponzi scheme."

The incomes of Wall Street CEOs were staggering; in 1992 and 1993, for example, the CEO of Bear Stearns, Jimmy Cayne, was earning $15 million a year. This greed would eventually catch up with many CEOs in the 2007 financial crash.

The risk of default was increasing; in 1996, Lehman Brothers and Bear Stearns became Wall Street's most highly leveraged firms, borrowing $32 for every $1 the firms had in capital.

In 1998, Jamie Dimon, CEO of J.P. Morgan, created Citigroup with partner Sandy Weill; this was the largest financial services organisation in the world. It operated in 107 countries, with 22,000 offices worldwide. It was valued at $640 billion, the largest merger during an era of mega merges; the deal was technically illegal because of the Glass-Steagall Act, which prevented investment banks from combining with commercial banks. Through powerful lobby groups, Weill sought to unwind it. The act was abolished one year later. Citigroup's massive balance sheet, the size of its deposits and cash on hand, came close to $3 trillion, the size of a small country's GDP.

The expansion of the mortgage loan market hit full throttle with the killing of the Glass-Steagall Act (the former separation of investment banks and commercial banks). The federal government, through the Federal Deposit Insurance Corporation, insured bank deposits up to $250,000.

Key point: In effect, the federal government and hence taxpayers were subsidising the risk-taking activities of the big banks, such as Citigroup.

In March 2000, trillions of dollars in wealth was destroyed when the NASDAQ—the market where most of the securities traded—fell from over 5000 points to just under 1500 points one year later. The economy was spluttering, and then the second shot was fired with the 9/11 terrorist attacks, which closed down Wall Street for one week. Fear of a total collapse of the economy spread, so Alan Greenspan did what FED chairmen have always done: He began slashing rates.

Now with historically low interest rates, which lasted until 2004, the housing bubble continued to grow. The rates amazingly went from

13 percent in 1981 to 1 percent in 2001. Banks wanted far more customers, so they dropped the 20 percent deposit requirement for mortgage applicants and opened their coffers to people who had little or no credit history. The so-called sub-prime (below par) mortgage, once a backwater in the banking industry, became a standard tool to lend money. Fanny Mae and Freddie Mac (government-sponsored enterprises) consequently started to ramp up their guarantees of sub-prime loans.

How did the banks profit more? The magic of securitisation: the slicing and dicing of various types of loans, credit cards, auto loans, and mortgages. These were repackaged into bonds. This allowed banks to keep on lending at levels they could only dream about. *Why not?* they thought. *We will simply sell our loans to Wall Street, who will package them into mortgage bonds and sell them to other investors.*

Now because a lot of Americans were so strapped for cash, they were using home equity loans for living expenses. These loans were treated like giant piggy banks. They were getting a mortgage, which incredibly was 120 percent of the value of their house. This brought in some creative applications for loans; with a few adjustments, any deadbeat could be transformed into someone who deserved a new and expensive home; in reality, they were liar loans.

Key point: The heart of the problem was the problem of the human heart.

Jeremiah said, "The heart of man is desperately wicked" (Jeremiah 31:33). There would come a time, however, when God's laws would be put into the human heart.

Now with more money chasing fewer loans, housing prices soared, even in working-class suburbs. Lending to high-risk borrowers meant the banks could ramp up fees and interest rates on their loans. These higher interest rates had another effect: They increased the returns of the mortgage-backed bonds that were created from these high-yielding sub-prime loans.

By 2005, the credit default swap essentially covered the cost of a bond if it fell into default. In reality, it had become the glue that held together the mortgage-backed securities markets. The cheap money supplied by the Federal Reserve created a bonanza of risk taking never seen before.

By early 2006, collateralised debt obligations (CDOs) and other bonds packed with sub-prime mortgages were starting to receive a chilly reception from investors. A CDO is a security backed by a pool of debt securities, not just limited to mortgages. A CDO is typically divided into various risk categories, which are then sold to investors.

Note: The inherent weakness of mortgage-backed bonds was, they could become toxic when interest rates rose or when people either prepaid their mortgages or defaulted on their payments.

The Fed and SEC did not even raise a peep when the massive and vapid build-up of mortgage debt by the banks approached $1 trillion by 2006. They were meant to be the nation's early warning system. It was like Nero fiddling while Rome burned. To compound the problem, the combined balance sheets of the government-sponsored enterprises grew by an average 15 percent per year, from $1.4 trillion in 1995 to $4.9 trillion in 2007 ($1 trillion of this was sub-prime).

Wall Street's avarice would eventually play a big part in their own demise. In early 2007, based on record profits of 2006, Goldman Sachs, Morgan Stanley, Merrill Lynch, Lehman Brothers, and Bear Stearns doled out $60 million in bonuses.

Now we come to another financially engineered product: structured investment vehicles (SIVs). SIVs are large pools of investment assets that were kept off the balance sheets of many banks. SIVs were funded by selling short-term debt to investors to finance the purchase of higher yielding long-term debt. The result was banks feasted on a regulatory gimmick that allowed them to take an enormous risk without a hint of disclosure or the expenditure of capital to cushion losses.

Underlying problems of the mortgage market were lax regulation, the expansion of the welfare state into the mortgage business, and the blindness of the credit rating agencies Standard and Poor's and Moody's. The SEC, which was supposed to be monitoring the capital lenders at the investment banks, was clueless to the now-emerging fact that the buildup of the risky assets was so huge that they did not have enough capital to cover their losses with investment banks, and commercial banks were being allowed to mix mortgage bond trading with savings deposits (because the Glass-Steagall Act had been struck down). The Federal Reserve even missed the massive buildup of loans. The banks were really ill prepared for the coming economic disaster.

Since we have talked about collateral debt obligations, here is a layman's description: It is like a stew of many different bonds, their main ingredient being mortgage bonds consisting of sub-prime loans and other backed securities. These CDOs were toxic time bombs just waiting to go off. Merrill Lynch, for example, held tens of billions of dollars of CDOs, for which there were no bids (unless you consider cents on the dollar to be a bid).

The end began in late February 2008, when AIG made a shocking announcement: It had lost $5.3 billion. This was its largest loss in history, a direct result of massive write-downs in losses stemming from its insurance of CDOs. Meredith Whitney, a relatively unknown analyst working for a second-tier firm, was one of the few people to predict the coming financial meltdown. She targeted Citigroup; her view was that Citigroup would have to unload $100 billion of assets to make up for losses and lower revenues. In a shrewd strategy, banks such as Merrill Lynch and Citigroup sought insurance as a way to keep risky assets on their books at full value, especially buying the triple A ratings of the insurers and placing them on their mortgage-backed bonds.

An example of mortgage-backed fraud (known later as liar loans) was a man whose application stated he was earning $70,000 USD per annum, for a consulting firm called Corum, and he had savings of $30,000. In reality, he had stated he was earning $30,000 per annum as an orderly in a hospital, and he had $1,400 in savings. He had to sell all his furniture a few months after the loan was taken out to meet his mortgage payment, which had ballooned out.

In an era of low interest rates and easy money, the banks never checked on whether the documentation submitted by the broker was real—and why should they? The loan was not its problem because it would be sold to Citigroup, Bear Stearns, or some other bank, which would package it into a mortgage-backed bond. As I mentioned earlier, this process was known as securitisation. It was later payback on the various banks that had demanded products for their bonds, thus spurring on lower lending standards that led people to receiving loans that they collected but never repaid. These sub-prime loans were way below par.

Black Friday was the day of reckoning; the global financial crisis started to bite when Bear Stearns's forty thousand shell-shocked employees found that the firm had been sold for a paltry $2 a share. Market analysts finally concluded that Bear's massive leverage and $30 billion in risky mortgage debt, now trading at cents in the dollar, was the final straw. It would have left the firm insolvent, even without the poor management. In reality, the hedge funds sparked a run-on Bear by drawing out their prime brokerage balances; the fire simply spread to all aspects of the market.

By the summer of 2008, the financial crisis had become a horror show. The bond rating agency Standard and Poor's clearly had not understood the complexity and flows of the CDOs and was now playing catch-up. They had to admit that 85 percent, or $285 billion, formerly triple A-rated CDOs issued in 2004 to 2006 could fall into default.

It also became clear that the federal government would have to bail out the government-sponsored enterprises. Countrywide had already been put out of its misery, having been purchased by the Bank of America as it careened towards bankruptcy.

The problem with CDOs was, they were jammed with so much debt (e.g., the case of Merrill Lynch) that they were almost impossible to value, so when push came to shove, they would have sold for almost nothing. Mortgage-backed bonds did not fare much better; Citigroup itself had it written down $40 billion in losses by August 2008.

The side effect of the anticipated Lehman Brothers implosion was that banks would not give small businesses loans to pay their workers before revenue came in, based on fears that there would be mass selling of assets. The crunch came on Tuesday, September 9, 2008, when the shares of Lehman were in free fall. By the time the day was over, Lehman shares were down 45 percent, as investors debated their final survival. Merrill Lynch was also going down, in tandem with Lehman. The moral hazard that the government had created by bailing out Long-Term Capital Management and then Bear Stearns was now manifesting itself.

The bottom line was, Wall Street had created the mess it was in; it had lost the confidence of the market through excessive risk taking and outright lying about its financial health, and Wall Street, not the government, had to find a solution.

Lehman's bankruptcy would haunt policymakers, as it became clear the downside of creating a moral hazard is that in so doing, they could add fuel to the financial panic. Amazingly, no one, from the Federal Reserve chairman to the treasurer and its employees, had predicted the size and magnitude of the crash that eventually came.

The financial system was in unchartered waters, something not seen in the lifetimes of the men who ran the world's big banks. The policymakers biggest worry was to prevent a full-scale collapse of the financial system, then the global economy, resulting in a crisis worse than the 1929 Great Depression. In this scenario, no one lends, no one trades, and unemployment shoots through the roof.

Nothing in American society had lost more credibility than Wall Street. For the past twenty-five years, it had consistently expanded on its risk taking, despite obvious signs that would lead to disaster; the remaining CEOs of Wall Street said their businesses were fine, but no one in the public believed them.

As I said before, the root cause of this malaise was greed. Businesses had rewarded excessive risk taking with higher and higher bonuses and consequently penalised those who came to Wall Street to simply make a good living. On Monday, September 15, 2008, the Dow Jones dropped five hundred points, the largest decline since the first day of trading following the 9/11 terrorist attacks.

The vultures circled; one of these was Barclay's, which bought Lehman's investment bank that Monday for about $1 a share, for $1.75 billion. The next grave concern was AIG, which sold life insurance to average Americans, but much more than that: It had been the glue that held the financial system together. Why? Because the biggest financial institutions had hedged their bonds by insurance, through (you guessed it) AIG. Now if AIG went under, Goldman Sachs wouldn't be far behind, nor would every other bank in the world, so Ben Bernanke of the Federal Reserve gave AIG the $85 billion it needed to survive, in exchange for a 79.9 percent stake in the insurer and onerous rates for the money.

Bernanke could not get his $700 billion spending plan through, and in the wake of a no vote, on September 30, 2008, the share market lost 777 points (the largest one-day decline in history). The run-on banks continued, so Goldman Sachs and Morgan Stanley did the unthinkable: They applied to become commercial banks. This meant they had direct access to the complete array of Federal Reserve emergency borrowing programs, which they did not have as investment banks. The Federal Reserve accepted that Wall Street was finished. They had to ditch the risk-taking model that had made them so much money over the last two decades. The avarice was unbelievable; never again would a CEO be able to earn more than $50 million for one day's work, as in the case of John Mack of Morgan Stanley and Lloyd Blankfein of Golden Sachs.

The only solution decided by the government was to direct investment into the affected financial firms by the Federal Reserve. The big banks got the most money: Citigroup, Bank of America, and J.P. Morgan Chase received $25 billion each. Morgan Stanley and Golden Sachs would get $10 billion each; in exchange, the government would eventually become part owners through a convertible share arrangement.

Amazingly, that was not the end of these handouts; in November, Treasury Secretary Henry Paulson along with Bernanke injected another $20 billion into Citigroup. The bottom line was, the US taxpayer was on the road to becoming the largest shareholder in one of the biggest, most distressed, and worst-run banks in US history.

The global economy had come so close to a complete financial meltdown, which included two investment banks blowing up, one-third forced into a merger, billions of dollars in shareholder value destroyed, and a titanic destruction of the wealth of average Americans. The Dow Jones Industrial Average had fallen from its October 2007 high of around 14,000 points, to around 6500 points in March 2009.

My latest research at the time of this writing is that there is going to be a systemic financial meltdown greater than the 2008 global financial crisis. The catalyst may be the sudden removal of millions of Christians from the earth, which is found in 1 Thessalonians 4:16–17. This will create unprecedented havoc to our economies. The dollar will collapse, millions will panic into buying gold, and there will only be a small window of opportunity for private investors to buy gold. The price of gold will soar, so I highly recommend that gold should be a part of everyone's wealth preservation strategy.

In part 4 of this book, "Personal Prosperity," we will look at proven ways to safeguard yourself from the bubble that is yet to burst.

PART 4

Personal Prosperity

We have looked at the macro view of prosperity and the global financial system, with its flawed quantitative easing (printing $4 trillion of money), which made only the top 0.1 percent of Americans, 156,000 people, earn average incomes of $5.6 million. Now we will look at proven strategies (that they never could teach you in college or high school). I have gone through the university of hard knocks, and I am so glad to share, through experience and research, the pitfalls to avoid. Common sense is not very common, and we could all do with some more, when it comes to money and what to do with it once we have it.

Key point: Winning at money, earning money, and keeping it is 80 percent behaviour and 20 percent head knowledge.

If you live a life of altruism (concern for the welfare of others), you can become debt free, enjoy a wonderful feeling of well-being, and give more to your fellow man than you ever thought possible. You have to take responsibility for your own life; it is not up to your children or your spouse. They will help, but the bottom line is the principles that you build your life on will determine how you live your retirement years. It is not just the quantity of years (we will look at how this is obtained in part 5, "Excellent Health"), but the quality of what is meant to be your golden years. Personal prosperity definitely involves close friends, a loving spouse (if married), and children you can be proud of. You may have heard of this truism: "People don't plan to fail, they just fail to plan." Wealth creation and legal tax minimisation is not for financially unfit people (if you don't use it, you will lose it).

Credit cards have become a way of life; in fact, Americans owe a total of $900 billion, but how did people manage before the plethora of credit cards hit our Western economy? I am going to apply some old-fashioned principles to our high-tech, so-called sophisticated way of living:

"The rich rules over the poor, and the borrower is servant to the lender" (Proverbs 22:7 NKJV).

Key point: If your home is way too big, downsize to something smaller. Jesus said…"Take heed and beware of covetousness, for one's life does not consist in the abundance of the things he possesses." (Luke 12:15 NKJV)

Try it; you will actually be happier with that greatly reduced mortgage and experience less stress and wonderful health benefits. Spend less than you make, spend only when you have cash, and do not borrow. If you have to use a credit card for Internet purchases or holiday bookings, make that the exception, provided you have the cash to pay out the credit card balance in full at the end of the month. Do an expenses spreadsheet (by ledger, binder, or computer), so you can see your outgoings at a glance. Typical headings would be rent/mortgage, housekeeping, car costs (including registration and insurance), home maintenance, cash out (for all small items), health and life insurance, education, social (includes holidays), and charity (church offerings come out of cash out). Every three months, do a subtotal times 4 divided by 52, and that weekly amount goes into a new budget summary under the headings; do this at the end of March, June, September, and December.

Here is an example chart:

Date	Week #	Net Income	Total	Expenses	Total	Difference	Average per week
7/7	1	$900	$900	$860	$860	$40 CR	$40 CR
14/7	2	$850	$1,750	$700	$1,560	$190 CR	$95 CR
21/7	3	$920	$2,670	$1,200	$2,760	$90 DR	$30 DR

Note: Do not wait for the start of the financial year; start after the completion of three months, as above. After six months, do another subtotal on each heading times 2 divided by 52 to get a clearer picture of your weekly expenses; this information came from your budget that you previously set up. At the end of twelve months, you will know exactly what is happening with your final totals.

Key point: Do not loan money to friends or relatives; it will strain the relationship. Just give it with no strings attached; you will both be much happier without damaging the relationship.

The bottom line is, new habits are hard to make, but once made, they are hard to break.

The average millionaire buys a two-year-old car, where all the kinks have been ironed out, and they keep away from car payments.

Note: Payments should be made on something that is appreciating, like a home or investment property (where you get tax deductions), not on a car, especially a new car, where the depreciation is severe in the first two years: A new car loses 60 percent of its value after four years. Do not lease a car; consumer experts have proved it is the most expensive way to operate a vehicle.

Now back to credit cards: 60 percent of people do not pay off their credit cards every month. If you must have a credit card for Internet purposes, then have a very low available balance, but pay everything else with your money. If you feel the temptation is too great, then cancel your credit card and only use a debit card; make cash and Internet payments from your savings account.

You cannot borrow your way out of debt. Debt is a symptom of overspending and under-saving. The banks know eventually you will spend more than you earn using your credit card (or cards), and it is the compound interest (interest on interest) that eventually cripples you and puts you over peak debt. Compound interest is great if you are the one receiving it. If you live within your means, saving and investing would cause wealth to be built up at an unprecedented level, which would create more stability and spending. Debt spending causes more families to break up and increases the burden on an overburdened government, unable to pay the interest payments on its ballooning debt. If families were debt free, donations and giving would increase, and many social problems would be privatised; consequently, the government would get out of the welfare business. Debt is not a tool; it is a method to make banks wealthy and not you. The borrower truly is a slave to the lender. The solution is found in 2 Corinthians 8:12–14, which basically says that if you have plenty and someone else is in need, you should give to them. It is an open display of God's love.

Part 5 is on how to have excellent health because the number one cause of bankruptcy is medical bills (number two is credit card debt).

The school system does not teach us how to manage money. Ignorance, not knowing how to handle money, and not a lack of intelligence is the problem. We now have tens of thousands of educated derelicts. This section will go a long way to address the problem based on someone who has gone through the university of hard knocks. I sincerely hope this will help you avoid the financial booby traps and debt time bombs waiting to go off. Your personal goal should be to aim for a zero-based budget, that is, income minus outgoings equals zero. Deficit spending has got the US government into serious financial trouble and is past the point of no return; do not let it happen to you on a personal level. Start an emergency fund now. It is not for buying things or for holidays; it is for emergencies. Christmas is not an emergency. The emergency fund should be equal to three months' expenses.

We must not continue doing the same thing over and over; if it is not working for you, then it is time for a change. We have to change what got us into this financial mess and simply do things differently. Experts say it takes twenty-one days to form a habit, whether good or bad. Your financial goal must include helping other people. There is power in numbers; we need each other's skills and support to succeed. It is very helpful in planning for success by writing down your goals and keeping them somewhere handy where you can see them. I have financial goals typed and stuck on the walls of my study, so the goals get reinforced every time I go in there.

The number one cause of divorce in America is money problems. If you consistently adhere to these strategies, you will remove this problem, which will allow you to bond with your spouse and friends and build healthy relationships. It is very satisfying to be able to help your friends financially and socially, once you have your debts under control.

A financial magazine stated that 78 percent of us would have a major negative event in a ten-year period of time. The first step is to start an emergency fund of $1,000 cash, building up to three months of your living expenses. If you do not know that figure, start doing a budget immediately.

Yes, it will be a sacrifice for many of you to plan ahead and have an emergency fund with cash that will cover any future mishaps, but it will be well worth it. Peace of mind alone is a wonderful experience.

Key point: Trusting God, timing, patience, and preparation will all result in financial peace. So if a real emergency happens, you can handle it with your emergency fund. No more borrowing; you have to break that cycle.

It is easy to become wealthy, if you do not have all those payments. So let's start the snowball strategy of debt reduction. First, list all your debts, in order of the smallest to pay off to the largest. The reason we start with the smallest is to have some quick wins; it is very satisfying and builds up your confidence. Now, you make the minimum payment to stay current on all debts, except the smallest one, which you pay off completely. Once the smallest debt is paid, any surplus money is used to pay off the next-smallest debt. When debt number two is paid off, you take the money that you used to pay on debt number one and debt number two, and pay it on debt number three. When debt number three is paid, you attack debt number four, and so on. When you get the impulse to buy something, a take-away meal or DVD, don't. It will be difficult but well worth it. Every time you pay one debt off, you will have more money left to pay the next debt, just like a snowball rolls over and picks up more snow and gets larger. By the time you get to the bottom, you have an avalanche.

Key point: Why on earth would you marry someone you don't trust? Your job is to love each other, and that includes having shared financial goals, which is hard to do when you have separate accounts.

A well-designed financial plan will walk you out of debt forever. Although a typical family can make $4,000 a month in Australia, how would you like to have a fully funded $13,000 emergency fund, and no payments but the mortgage? If you get laid off or your car engine blows up, you don't have to rely on credit cards. Make it standard practise to refill your emergency fund as soon as possible. It will save you from a lot of hard times and prevent further debt.

A national financial survey found, that 49 percent of Americans would only be able to cover less than one month's expenses if they lost their income. Remember: Something that is on a sale is not an emergency.

Note: A fixed-term deposit account is not to be used as an emergency fund, as it has penalties if you withdraw before the time. It has to be liquid, like an on-call Internet savings account, which usually beats the main banks in paying out interest.

Your mission statement for your emergency fund should be to protect you from the storms of life, give you peace of mind, and keep the next problem from getting you further into debt. Every emergency should not be a faith project, although God can move on somebody to give you money, but that is not His best for your life. Remember: It should be big enough to cover three to six months' expenses.

The riskier your situation is, for example, commission selling, the greater your emergency fund should be. Most families take twenty-four to thirty months to get three to six months' expenses saved, and then they start some serious accumulation of wealth. No more debt, except for the home mortgage. Your goal now is to be wealthy enough to give to charities, retire with dignity, leave an inheritance, and also be able to enjoy yourself in your golden years.

"A good man leaves an inheritance to his children's children, but the wealth of the sinner is stored up for the righteous" (Proverbs 13:22 NKJV).

Maximise Retirement

Retirement success does not mean saving enough money to quit a job you hate; do not wait until you turn sixty-five to do what you love. You need a plan where your money works harder than you do. The golden rule in retirement is to invest 15 percent of your gross income into your industry super fund, which has a lower fee than a retail fund.

Key point: Do not include the 9.5 percent superannuation guaranteed charge in your calculations (that is, the compulsory super for employees). Also, do not use your potential Social Security benefits in your calculations. If Social Security is not there, or greatly diminished, you will be glad you took my advice. The upside is that if Social Security is available, it is a bonus, and you will be able to help charities of your choice.

It is never too late to start. George Burns won his first Oscar at eighty. Gold Meir was prime minister of Israel at seventy-one. Albert Schweitzer was still performing surgery in Africa at age eighty-nine. Statistics show that fifty-four out of a hundred people aged sixty-five years old will still have to work because of the lack of money; don't be one of them.

Now, let's look at Australian retirees figures as of Feb 2016:

Age Pension Eligibility

Date of Birth	Qualifying Age
July 1, 1952, to December 31, 1953	65.5
January 1, 1954, to June 30, 1955	66
July 1, 1955, to December 31, 1956	66.5
From January 1, 1957	67

Centrelink, an office of the Department of Human Services (DHS), is responsible for payments and other services related to the Social Security system. The age pension is subject to a means test. Centrelink applies both an income and assets test. The test which generates the lowest pension is the one that is used.

Income Test for Full Pension

Singles are allowed $162 per fortnight and couples $288 per fortnight.

Income Test for Part Pension

Once singles reach $162 per fortnight in income, pensions reduce by 50 cents per dollar on the amount over $162. Once couples reach $288 per fortnight in income, pensions reduce by 25 cents per dollar on the amount over $288.

Note: The net retail earnings from real estate investments is included in the income test. I highly recommend an accountant for any investment property you may have.

It is impossible for Centrelink to work out all the investment returns, so they have brought out a deeming rate to cover everyone. For a single person, the first $48,600 is deemed to be earning 1.75 percent; for amounts above $48,600, the deeming rate is 3.25 percent. For a couple, the first $80,600 is deemed to be earning 1.75 percent; for amounts above $80,600, the deeming rate is 3.25 percent. The amount calculated is then added to any income from personal labour, that is, part-time income, commissions, and so on.

Now, let's look at the asset test:

	Maximum Assets for No Reduction	Assets (No Pension over These Amounts)
Single Homeowner	$205,500	$779,000
Single Nonhomeowner	$354,500	$928,000
Couple Homeowner	$291,500	$1,156,500
Couple Nonhomeowner	$440,500	$1,305,500

Your fortnightly pension is reduced $1.50 per $1,000 above the no reduction amount

Please note: Your family home is not counted in the assets test, but your car is and household contents like beds, TVs, and furniture.

The 2015 federal budget stated that in January 2017, there will be significant changes in the assets test, which will affect the single and couple pension. Here are some examples which will give you a snapshot of how it could affect you:

	September 2015 Pension		January 2017 Pension	
Assessable Assets	Single	Couples	Single	Couples
$100,000	$867.00	$1,307.00	$891.00	$1,343.20
$250,000	$800.25	$1,307.00	$891.00	$1,343.20
$300,000	$725.25	$1,294.75	$741.00	$1,343.20
$400,000	$575.25	$1,144.25	$441.00	$1,268.20
$500,000	$425.25	$994.25	$141.00	$968.20
$547,000	$354.75	$923.75	$0.00	$827.20
$650,000	$200.25	$769.25	$0.00	$518.20
$750,000	$50.25	$619.25	$0.00	$218.20
$800,000	$0.00	$544.25	$0.00	$68.20
$823,000	$0.00	$509.75	$0.00	$0.00
$900,000	$0.00	$394.25	$0.00	$0.00
$1,000,000	$0.00	$244.25	$0.00	$0.00
$1,100,000	$0.00	$94.25	$0.00	$0.00
$1,200,000	$0.00	$0.00	$0.00	$0.00

Please note: The pension is paid fortnightly.

Key point: If you spend money on your home, your assessable assets, that is, money in the bank, goes down, and your pension would go up. For example, if you spend $100,000 on home improvements and your assessable assets went from $500,000 to $400,000, your pension would increase from $141 to $441 (for a single person) in 2017. That is net $7,800 per annum; for a couple, it would go from $968.20 to $1,268.00 per fortnight.

I was a life insurance broker before I was an investment consultant; the insurance industry has a pretty good idea how many years on an average you have to live. This knowledge may spur you on to start saving sooner rather than later. So let's look at your life expectancy.

How Long Have You Got?
Life Expectancy (Years to Live)

Age	Male	Female
50	31.43	35.17
55	26.95	30.53
60	22.63	26.00
65	18.54	21.62
70	14.76	17.42
75	11.31	13.51
80	8.38	10.01
85	6.03	7.08
90	4.36	4.91
95	3.36	3.53
100	2.81	2.74

How to Manage Your Wealth

Now, here is a truism: "College degrees certainly do not insure success." Your college degree will only produce for you if you mix knowledge with the right attitude, character, perseverance, vision, diligence, conscientiousness, and a commitment to work. Wisdom is much more than passing a series of tests; it is the skilful application of knowledge.

Student debt is crippling this current generation, so stay away from loans and make plans to stop borrowing. In America, the average student loan debt is $26,000. That is $36,000 in Australian dollars.

How did previous generations of university students do it? Well, they lived with relatives, slept in dormitories, ate cafeteria food, and worked part time wherever possible. I worked at nights to put myself through Bible college and support two young children as well.

Now, back to the homeowners who are getting financially fit in this marathon. The next baby step is to pay off your mortgage. Every dollar you can find above living, college, and retirement planning should be used to make extra payments on your mortgage.

Key point: Take out the shortest mortgage in years (for example, fifteen and not thirty years). You are fooling yourself if you take out a thirty-year mortgage so you can make extra monthly payments. Research has shown almost no one does this. Pretend only a fifteen-year mortgage exists. Keep your investing very simple; keep away from unnecessary stress by getting into complex investments like options trading.

The Bible states in Proverbs 11:14 (NKJV), "Where there is no counsel, the people fall; but in the multitude of counsellors there is safety."

Essential members of your team include a CPA, an insurance professional, an investment professional, and a good estate planning lawyer.

So when your money makes more than you do, you are officially wealthy. You will find that giving is possibly the most enjoyable thing you will do with money. Recreation is good, but you will tire of golf and travel, and if you keep eating too much crayfish, it will eventually start tasting like soap. Investing is good, but like going around and around the Monopoly board, it eventually loses its appeal. I talked with millionaires as an investment manager of Westpac, and the common thread was that giving was the greatest joy. The Bible says that it is better to give than to receive. The creator was right all along. The Bible also says pure religion is actually helping the poor, not theorising about why they are poor.

James 1:27 (NKJV) says, "Pure and undefiled religion before God and the Father is this: to visit orphans and widows in their trouble, and to keep oneself unspotted from the world."

The bottom line is, all the stuff in the world can't compare to the feeding and helping of others in need. The three uses of money are recreation, investing, and giving.

Key point: Proverbs 10:22 (NKJV) says, "The blessing of the LORD makes one rich, and He adds no sorrow with it."

Wealth brings commitment and responsibility. Wealth has brought sorrow where it has become a god to them. It is our attitude towards our wealth that matters to God because our attitude will determine how we manage our possessions.

Keys to Your Personal Prosperity

In my study on traits of Godly, successful people, they all have one thing in common: They were very reticent to spend money on themselves. Their spiritual disciplines involved prayer, diligence, faithfulness, integrity, purity, servanthood, and financial stewardship. Their economic disciplines included time management, wise spending, hard work, and debt restraint.

I mentioned giving just recently, so try giving something away and enjoy the blessings you will receive. You will receive happiness, hope, a sense of peace, and well-being. When my friends and I give to the poor on the streets of Perth, we always come away happy.

Matthew 25:21 (NKJV) says, "His lord said to him, 'Well done, good and faithful servant; you were faithful over a few things, I will make you ruler over many things. Enter into the joy of your lord.'"

A steward is responsible for the interest of another; the essential quality of a steward is faithfulness. When we are faithful, God gives us more because we have proven that we are diligent to use what He gives us with wisdom and generosity.

Let's see what the word of God has to say about your prosperity.

God wants to give you good things and increase your business:

"For You, Lord, are good, and ready to forgive, and abundant in mercy to all those who call upon You" (Psalm 86:5 NKJV).

God wants you to have success and prosperity:

"For You meet him with the blessings of goodness; You set a crown of pure gold upon his head" (Psalm 21:3 NKJV).

God gives you power to get wealth:

"And you shall remember the LORD your God, for it is He who gives you power to get wealth, that He may establish His covenant which He swore to your fathers, as it is this day" (Deuteronomy 8:18).

God wants to bless your work:

"The LORD will open to you His good treasure, the heavens, to give the rain to your land in its season, and to bless all the work of your hand. You shall lend to many nations, but you shall not borrow" (Deuteronomy 28:12 NKJV).

God wants to make your work increase and prosper:

"The LORD your God will make you abound in all the work of your hand, in the fruit of your body, in the increase of your livestock, and in the produce of your land for good. For the LORD will again rejoice over you for good as He rejoiced over your fathers" (Deuteronomy 30:9 NKJV).

God has the power to create something from nothing:

"For He spoke, and it was done; He commanded, and it stood fast" (Psalm 33:9 NKJV).

The bottom line is, rescue your life and liberate your future by starting to give to others.

In April 2016, a woman appeared as a guest on *It's Supernatural*, a TV show hosted by Sid Roth. She was trying to get a church going. She and her husband were struggling financially, and her two children were chronically ill. They desperately prayed, and God showed them to take their only $5 and buy food and put it into brown paper bags and go on the streets and give it to the poor. God moved on people's hearts to help them. They were able to buy a used car yard, which started to prosper in 2011, while others around them were going bust, and their two children were able to get off their medication. She went from the Old Covenant formula tithe to the New Covenant of relationship. Torben Sondergaard, the Norwegian evangelist who has posted dozens of sermons on Youtube called "The Last Reformation/ Pioneer School," found the same thing.

Now some practical advice is, we have to get back to an attitude of paying cash. When you pay cash, you will buy less, and you will pay less. Research has shown that consumers purchase one-third less when paying with cash. When you use credit, you don't always pay it off at the end of the month, so you consequently pay more. The bottom line is, you severely restrict your ability to save and invest if there is debt hanging over your head.

So these are the advantages of paying cash:

- You will not be an impulse buyer, like when using credit.
- You will attempt to purchase at a discount price, so as to spend less if you use cash.
- You will not have to worry about destroying your planned budget.
- You will have peace of mind, and your purchases will be more satisfying when you use cash.

Key point: It is much better to fund your dreams instead of serving your debt.

If you don't have the cash, then walk away. If you want to freeze the level of debt, then freeze spending. In other words, simply live below your means. Most people do not have an income problem; they have a spending problem. Remember: The quality of your retirement is not up to your government; it is up to you.

Successful people share the following traits:

- If you will live like no one else now, you can live like no one else later.
- They live below their means.
- They allocate their money, free time, and energy to wealth accumulation.
- They carefully select occupations that complement their skills and talents, which leads to building wealth.
- They buy a two-year-old car instead of a new car, where all the problems have been sorted out, and save on the massive two-year devaluation.
- They do not live extravagant lives.

Successful people have learned important lessons about living on a budget and accounting for their expenses. I have an expense spreadsheet and pay close attention to all expenses. It is a good idea to pay yourself first, 10 percent of your income. That is, save it and invest it, and adjust your lifestyle accordingly. People discount it because it seems too simple, yet the compounding of income is so effective.

Note well: Living beyond your means creates high stress levels, and that affects your health, your spiritual life, your marriage, and your financial life. Living below your means actually decreases the normal stress of life; it will give you more peace. You will enjoy life more, make far better decisions, and have more time to be in touch with your creator. This peace shows; it flows to your spirit, soul, and body. This is how you will fulfil: "Now may the God of peace Himself sanctify you completely; and may your whole spirit, soul, and body be preserved blameless at the coming of our Lord Jesus Christ" (1 Thessalonians 5:23 NKJV).

So the bottom line is, you may give up a little of your spending power now, but by doing so, you will yield a whole lot more later.

A good start would be to do without some things that you would normally buy; it could be that daily latte or a fast food snack, or convert unneeded, unused possessions into cash. You know what they say: "One man's trash is another man's treasure."

Deficit spending must stop; the debt must be paid, and savings must begin. Here are some reasons to motivate you to stay within a planned budget, pay off the debt, and keep it paid off:

To Stay Physically Healthy

Debt can cause stress, sickness, depression, illness, and poor health.

To Stay Emotionally Healthy

Once the novelty or pleasure wears off on the new purchase, the payments keep coming, which can cause you further stress.

To Stay Mentally Healthy

The key to sound financial decisions is to have a clear mind that produces clarity of thought and judgement.

To Keep a Healthy Marriage

Have your finances under control and reduce that weight of debt, which inexorably grinds at you. Bad handling of finances has been said to be the number one cause of divorce. Good open communication and accountability strengthen the marriage.

To Have Money for Repairs

It is a wonderful feeling to have built up that emergency fund to cover those unexpected repair bills.

To Pay for Education without Adding More Debt

To be able to choose private education is a privilege, and careful planning will enable you to do this without going into more debt.

To Fulfil Dreams

Debt has a way of dashing our hopes, dimming our vision, and destroying our dreams.

To Enjoy Retirement

You want to enjoy retirement and not endure it. It's not just about longevity of life but a quality of life. You don't have to work ten years longer than your friends. Do you really need those long weekend trips away, a mansion, movies? Remember: Pay yourself 10 percent first and adjust your lifestyle. I know it can be discouraging to limit your wants and not enjoy a few extras as you have done in the past, but it will be well worth it, to see those debts knocked over one by one, starting with the smallest debt. Remember 1 Timothy 6:6: "Now godliness with contentment is great gain."

Key point: Value character over cash, do it God's way, and contentment will be your reward.

Debt hanging over you stifles your joy and creativity, and it does not give you time for your spiritual disciplines, daily devotions, scripture meditation, and praying for others.

Remember: If you don't have the money, do not spend. Credit is not your friend; it is your enemy. You certainly do not have to be old and in debt, and have little or nothing to show for it.

Here is a truism that has changed: Before the 2007 global financial crisis, it was said businesses have money but no time, and retired people have time but no money. Now it is most businesses, especially small businesses, that don't have time or money, and pensioners still have time but no money. People don't plan to fail; they just fail to plan. From your expenses spreadsheet, you should know every week what your personal cash flow is, either negative or positive from your budget.

This may come as a surprise to some, but you can enjoy life without spending money. Your attitude is more important than giftedness and is the harbinger of all skills needed for success and happiness.

We have to acknowledge who really owns what. God really owns me because He purchased me with His blood. I need to acknowledge His ownership; Revelation 4:11 (NKJV) says, "You are worthy, O Lord, to receive glory and honour and power; for You created all things and by Your will they exist and were created."

We all have a responsibility to work and to be good stewards of our gifts. If we are idle and lazy, we will be judged accordingly.

Ecclesiastes 10:18 (NKJV) says, "Because of laziness the building decays, and through idleness of hands the house leaks."

We must account for every idle word.

Matthew 12:36 (NKJV) says, "But I say to you that for every idle word men may speak, they will give account of it in the day of judgment."

What about idle time? Be productive.

We all have the responsibility to be productive, and when your days are full of productive tasks, you enjoy life more. As good stewards, we should work hard and go the extra mile, like the ant described in Proverbs 6:6–11. (NKJV).

The bottom line is, the ant has no one to tell it what to do: no supervisor, no overseer, and yet it is a self-starter and self-motivator. Time management is very important. God is the giver of time, and He has a right to expect us to use it wisely. Each day, you get 86,400 seconds; if you fail to use the day's deposits, the loss is yours. The word of God sums it up well in Ephesians 5:15–16 (NKJV):

(15) "See then that you walk circumspectly, not as fools but as wise, (16) redeeming the time, because days are evil."

It's not the days in your life but the life in your days."

Planning for the future is biblical. Joseph got the insight on storing wheat; he told the people of Egypt to prepare for the coming famine:

(48) "So he gathered up all the food of the seven years which were in the land of Egypt, and laid up the food in the cities; he laid up in every city the food of the fields which surrounded them.

(49) Joseph gathered very much grain, as the sand of the sea, until he stopped counting, for it was immeasurable." (Genesis 41:48–49 NKJV).

While we are able and in good health, we should be setting aside money as an emergency fund, in case there is a time of financial drought in our lives. The financial markets would have said Joseph's case was insider trading, but this time, it was legal and from God.

Sensible people look ahead and plan for the future. They manage money to provide for the present as well as the future. We, as stewards of Jesus Christ, are mandated with the responsibility to use every means at our disposal to spread the good news.

We all need disciplined living. The Western world has been blessed way above the third world countries. Those we consider poor by our standards would be rich by the standards of the rest of the world. For example, if you rent a house and have a car, you are in the top 7 percent of the world's population (504 million people). If you have a home and a car, you are in the top 5 percent (360 million people). Prior to 1929, 95 percent of purchases were in cash, and prior to 1945, almost all cars were paid for in cash; now, the average American has seven credit cards, a financed car, and a mortgaged home, and 72 percent of people never pay their credit card balances off.

Diligence Is a Cornerstone of Financial Success

"The desire of the lazy man kills him, for his hands refuse to labour.

He covets greedily all day long, but the righteous gives and does not spare" (Proverbs 21:25–26 NKJV).

Key point: Lazy people always find a reason for not finishing a job; they will always state the reason for doing nothing.

Here is a scripture which some say supports the tithe, but it has nothing to do with the tithe. Its purpose was for famine relief and for the poor Christians in Jerusalem:

"On the first day of the week let each one of you lay something aside, storing up as he may prosper, that there be no collections when I come.

And when I come, whomever you approve by your letters I will send to bear your gift to Jerusalem" (1 Corinthians 16:2–3 NKJV).

Our giving must be bountiful and with the knowledge that our kindness and generosity would help those in need. It is not the amount of the giving, but the motive of the giving is what God sees (1 Peter 5:5).

I learned the law of increase from a guest on *It's Supernatural*, hosted by Sid Roth. The Holy Spirit had shown him that when Peter obeyed Jesus and put the fishing net on the right side (word of knowledge from Jesus), he pulled up a boat-sinking load of fish. He called James and John, who had the other fishing boat, and filled their nets also. Now here is a wonderful revelation: If Peter had a hundred boats instead of two, then all hundred boats would have been filled. The bottom line is, when God owns your business, He will make sure it prospers.

Here is a strong word of caution: If you desire to be a millionaire and think it is going to bring you happiness, but don't desire to use that wealth to prosper God's kingdom, only to obtain more and more things (materialism), this will bring you unhappiness and anxiety.

Remember: Great wealth has great responsibility. There is a string of broken families and broken lives among the rich. Remember the pitiful life of Howard Hughes, who with all his money and power became miserable and crazed.

Maintain an Attitude of Gratitude

There is a reason God does not have many gospel entrepreneurs or gospel patrons: 95 percent of men and women who started out with the right motive, when they became extremely wealthy, changed gods and served money and not the living God. In the midst of prosperity, the challenge for believers is to handle wealth in such a way that it acts as a blessing and not a curse. Remember: Materialism is a fruitless attempt to find meaning outside of God.

Greed and selfishness come from a prideful heart (me first), and this puts a blockage between God and us. Our motive must be to help people in need; the bottom line is not the amount, but the motive. Remember 2 Corinthians 9:7: "Be a cheerful giver."

How much should you be saving? You have to take into account inflation of 3.2 percent per annum, so you should start with the habit of saving 15 percent of your take-home pay. Most psychologists state it takes twenty-one days to form a habit, whether good or bad.

Key point: Put 50 percent of your next salary increase into a separate investment account before it reaches your wallet.

Always remember: God uses many vehicles to get the job done, but in the end, it is not us but God's blessing upon our lives:

"And you shall remember the LORD your God, for it is He who gives you power to get wealth, that He may establish His covenant which He swore to your fathers, as it is this day" (Deuteronomy 8:18 NKJV).

Please note that when you partner with God in business, He will not only bless it, He will let you enjoy it:

"The blessing of the LORD makes one rich, and He adds no sorrow with it" (Proverbs 10:22 NKJV).

When we acknowledge that God owns everything, we realise we are all stewards. A steward is simply a manager of someone else's money and possessions. We gain by giving; we lose by withholding.

Note: The biblical mandate is to seek the kingdom first.

Believers' lives can be spoiled if they are completely absorbed in possessions and the pursuit of material accumulation. We must ask God to help us develop an attitude of serving Him faithfully and a life that is free of debt, so we can extend the kingdom priorities instead of our human desires. Our attitude should be to bless others, share our resources, and be altruistic (concerned for the welfare of others). When I was in direct selling, although I was earning a good income, the real joy came when there was an opportunity to pray for the sick and lead them to Christ. God will use us as a conduit to make the supernatural happen if we just step out and make ourselves available.

Long ago, we stepped out in faith and went full time in a home-based business. There were times when we did not have enough to eat; we prayed and saw God multiply our food. Supernatural provision happens when the natural is not enough; we needed help and God came through. It is not about what we have, but what has us (1 Kings 17:15–16).

Jesus understood perfectly that consumer culture would develop in the end times; yes, there is a battle for our affections, our hearts, and our souls. We need to be continuously praying and asking God where He would like us to put our money. You may be pleasantly surprised, as you will go from formula to relationship and become spoilt for the ordinary.

Real Wealth

One of the Bible principles is to be proactive: "The plans of the diligent lead surely to plenty, but those of everyone who is hasty, surely to poverty" (Proverbs 21:5 NKJV).

Steady plodding brings prosperity; hasty speculation brings poverty. In these volatile times, unless you have been professionally trained, keep away from the share market and currency trading. When we think of success, the majority of people think of having a lot of money. Real success is doing what God desires. You can't help the poor if you are one yourself; however, having more than enough is only part of true success. It is having a loving spouse, feeling the blessing of children who love and respect you, and enjoying great health and great relationships. Wealth is having good friends.

People will find happiness in the exact proportion to the degree in which they give. They will be content, and 1 Timothy 6:6 says, "Godliness with contentment is great gain." Riches do not bring contentment, but contentment has a higher value than money or possessions. Now the test and fruit of good stewardship is how we use our blessings.

It is disappointing that people can spend an entire lifetime trying to get rich, only to find that with millions of dollars in the bank, they are still unhappy, still dissatisfied with life, and still sad. It is as if they climbed to the top of the ladder, only to find that it was placed on the wrong wall.

The key is to ask the Holy Spirit each week how much to put into the offerings (go from the formula of the tithe to a relationship with the Holy Spirit). Do that also with charities you are supporting. Merilyn and I pray before we give anything to anybody and ask how much to give to the charities that we regularly support. The Christian must love God and not money, but use money prayerfully to expand God's kingdom. It has become a real joy since 1988, when I started out on Spirit-led giving.

This is a warning to not love money:

"But those who desire to be rich fall into temptation and a snare, and into many foolish and harmful lusts which drown men in destruction and perdition.

For the love of money is a root of all kinds of evil, for which some have strayed from the faith in their greediness, and pierced themselves through with many sorrows" (1 Timothy 6:9–10 NKJV).

Note: Our original first two parents of mankind, Adam and Eve, had everything, yet they were deceived into thinking that they needed more and gave in to the lying way of Satan, working through the serpent. The result was personal destruction for them and all mankind. Fortunately, Jesus, the second Adam, restored what was lost. If we would only get the Holy Spirit involved in our financial life, and took everything to our Lord in prayer, we would not have to bear needless pain.

We know that God has great plans for you and wants to bless you: "For I know the thoughts that I think toward you, says the LORD, thoughts of peace and not of evil, to give you a future and a hope" (Jeremiah 29:11 NKJV).

Both Jesus and Satan are very interested in what you do with your money. Our attitude towards money is a spiritual matter. If our attitude is right, we will be good stewards of all that God has allowed us to oversee. This will ensure that an unending supply will come our way. When we get God's plan, it is blessed; if we do things our own way, a lot of things seem to go wrong. It is a lot easier when God is in it.

It is nice to know that if we team up with God, He will allow us to keep some for ourselves. If your business is dedicated to God, it becomes His problem and not yours. So the bottom line is, possessions and money are not bad; in fact, they are good when used as tools to support the kingdom.

Do Not Overindulge

Proverbs 21:17 (NKJV) says, "He who loves pleasure will be a poor man; he who loves wine and oil will not be rich."

This verse tells us that the love of pleasure and overindulgence squanders assets and prevents us from building financial resources. Jesus summed it up perfectly in Luke 12:15 (NKJV): "And He said to them, 'Take heed and beware of covetousness, for one's life does not consist in the abundance of the things he possesses.'"

The spiritual problem comes with the love of things. The Christian way is all about servanthood and sacrifice, not materialism and overindulgence. I hope you can still see I want you to prosper, but keep a balance and still be focused on kingdom building, not buildings. God loves to see you prosper; look at Psalm 35:27 (NKJV): "Let them shout for joy and be glad, who favour my righteous cause; and let them say continually, 'Let the LORD be magnified, who has pleasure in the prosperity of His servant.'"

You become blessed so you can bless others.

Here are some key points to remember:

- God must be recognised as the source of all things.
- He must be credited full ownership of all you possess.
- We must know that our spiritual prosperity is infinitely more important than our material prosperity.

Now let's see: Colossians 3:23 (NKJV) says, "And whatever you do, do it heartily, as to the Lord and not to men."

This passage is telling believers that they must be diligent and focused on whatever God has told them to do. You may remember previously I said: Whatever the Holy Spirit tells you to do, do it; we must listen.

Fiscal Planning Is Very Important

People don't plan to fail; they fail to plan. We must plan our destiny with Godly wisdom (Proverbs 21:5).

Retirement Planning

Retirement planning is really just tomorrow thinking, but long term. As we have seen, we need to talk to God about it and obtain a successful strategy and vehicle. Now in the latter part of this section, we are going to look at a number of practical ways to free up some of your money and plan for retirement and wealth creation.

Let's look at the magic of compound interest. We have to be prepared for the havoc that inflation can play on our investments over the long term.

Investment Details

- interest rate compounded continuously
- weekly payments
- forty-five years of 2,340 payments of $25
- interest rate 10 percent

The Magic of Compound Interest to Combat Inflation

Age at Beginning of Investment	Investment Value at Age 55	Investment Value at Age 60	Investment Value at Age 65	Weekly Contribution
20	$417,902	$697,446	$1,158,336	$25
25	$248,351	$417,902	$697,446	$25
30	$145,512	$248,351	$417,902	$25
35	$83,138	$145,512	$248,351	$25
40	$45,305	$83,138	$145,512	$25
45	$22,359	$45,305	$83,138	$25
50	$8,441	$22,359	$45,305	$25

"Render therefore to all their due: taxes to whom taxes are due, customs to whom customs, fear to whom fear, honour to whom honour.

Owe no one anything except to love one another, for he who loves another has fulfilled the law" (Romans 13:7–8 NKJV).

Try not to borrow except for your home or your investment property, with all its tax advantages. The bottom line is, if you don't borrow, you can't get into debt.

What I am going to say now is not new: Show me a person who is deep in debt, and I will show you a person who feels in bondage. They work all day just to meet their payments, then they have to find money to live. They might try and get overtime, or get a second part-time job so they can keep afloat. Proverbs 22:7 (NKJV) says, "The rich rules over the poor, and the borrower is servant to the lender."

Financial Danger

What is financial danger? Becoming a slave to debt! 2 Peter 2:19 says, "While they promise them liberty, they themselves are slaves of corruption; for by whom a person is overcome, by him also he is brought into bondage."

Remember: What we are is far more important than what we possess. If you have any of these symptoms, you are already in too much debt:

- use a cash advance from one credit card to make payments on another.
- have less than two months' take-home pay in cash or savings where you can get at it quickly.
- have more than 15 percent of your take-home pay to credit payments (other than your mortgage).
- have overdue notices from creditors.

We have found the absolute essential requirement is to pray each day and ask God for His strategies so we can give into the kingdom of God. The Bible says, "As many as are led by the spirit of God are the children of God." Yes, we have a far superior New Covenant than the Old Covenant.

Lifestyle Change

There are only five things you are able to do with money: give it, save it, invest it, lend it, and spend it. Spending should never be the first thing you do with money. Save 10 percent first and adjust your lifestyle; it's not what you make but what you spend. Your attitude towards spending should be no debt, no matter what.

Here are some timely principles you should apply to your new lifestyle:

- A good rule for borrowing is never borrow for depreciating items.
- Debt is incurred because people want something before they have the money for it.

"Blessed is everyone who fears the LORD, who walks in His ways.

When you eat the labour of your hands, you shall be happy, and it shall be well with you" (Psalm 128:1–2 NKJV).

The key point here is, after you have prayed and given an offering to the work of the kingdom, pay yourself next. Do not just save it: Invest it or put it into your offset account or open an online savings account. An offset account is where your money reduces your mortgage balance for interest calculation purposes.

For example, if your mortgage is $400,000, your mortgage offset can be $10,000.

Interest is only charged on $390,000, yet you still have access to your $10,000. The interest is not taxed at your marginal rate of tax because it is in a tax-sheltered environment. Always remember that God, who gave you the talent, intelligence, and ability to think and work, is your source. All He asks is that you trust and obey the New Covenant. Those who demonstrate that they can be trusted with more will be blessed beyond what they desire or imagine.

A very important key is that you must do a budget. Budgets are not a record of expenses; they are a forecast of your expenses. Even if you have a budget, you still need to review it half-yearly to make sure that your spending habits are on track. It's you and God: "A man's heart plans his way, but the LORD directs his steps" (Proverbs 16:9 NKJV). The bottom line is, budgeting stops unnecessary spending.

Determine not to overspend; be wise in your spending. Isaiah 55:2 in the Living Bible says, "Why spend your money on food that doesn't give you strength? Why pay for groceries that do you no good?" In part 5, we will examine more closely foods that do harm and foods that help to heal.

You may be surprised when you keep track of where all your money is going. Those impulse-buying days will show up on your spreadsheet. At a glance, you will be able project future spending and saving. Review past saving and spending; see your cash flow in your Saturday-ending weekly cash flow. It will be either negative or positive. Control what you spend, and the pay-off is that you will be managing your money instead of your money managing you.

Once you are debt free, staying debt free has some wonderful benefits and certainly enhances your feeling of well-being. Here are some of the benefits:

- You invest competently and consistently.
- You turn away from impulsive behaviour.
- You borrow cautiously.
- You are financially prepared for the unexpected.

The bottom line is, living without debt is a lifestyle where you spend less than you earn, give, save, and invest with confidence and assurance.

It is better to aim at something and miss it than to aim at nothing and hit it.

Goals that do not include service to others will at best hinder and at worst destroy you. When I was an investment consultant for Westpac, I learned that being persistent and determined is far more valuable than raw talent; a lot of people with great talent are not living successful lives, and even education does not guarantee success. Persistence and determination alone are omnipotent. We need more decrees and fewer degrees to get the job done; life is much more than the ability to pass a series of tasks and examinations.

Keeping financial records is important; they may not provide answers to new problems, but they will reveal instantly how much money is available. Here is what I do: Every Saturday, rule off your last expense on your various accounts and credit card on your ledger (you can do this on your computer; at age sixty-seven, I am comfortable with hand writing in a ledger).

A weekly summary would look like this:

Date	Week #	Income	Total	Expenses	Total	Difference	CR or DR Amount per Week

You will know immediately what your weekly deficit spending is or later what your surplus average is. Yes, God can move on someone to make up the shortfall, but every week should not have to be a faith project.

A good debt-reduction strategy is like a snowball gathering momentum. Faster payments lower interest costs and allow you to own your home outright sooner. Obviously, a paid-up home is the cheapest way to live in retirement; for example, an extra $50 a month will significantly reduce your mortgage and pay your home off years earlier. On a $150,000 thirty-year 10 percent mortgage, you will save $68,325 and reduce the loan by more than five years. The fifty dollars coming straight off your principal, and the magic of compound interest in reverse, is a great help to you. (Unfortunately, rates will not stay at the current low over the next twenty-five years.)

Always ask yourself these four questions; they will not only lead to good spending habits but help you invest in yourself, to grow into your full potential:

- Can I really afford it?
- Do I really need it?

- Is it worth what I am paying for it?
- What is the most effective use of my time right now?

Another way of saving money is by doing things yourself, rather than paying someone else. Merilyn cuts my hair for me and looks after her own. She makes our bread in a bread-making machine and makes our ice cream in an ice cream maker; we also grow a lot of our fruit and vegetables in our back garden. Here are some things you can do in the personal choice category:

- Review insurance policies to avoid overlapping coverage.
- Always switch off the light when you leave the room.
- Turn power points off at the wall on appliances and TVs and so on.
- Buy a two-year-old car rather than a new one, if possible, because you will save a lot on depreciation, and it will be well run in and still have plenty of life left.
- Buy Christmas decorations after Christmas and save them for next year.
- Borrow books from your local library instead of buying new ones (the exception would be new Christian books that you can't get at the library).
- Start walking or jogging in the park and save on health club fees.
- Wash your car yourself instead of using a car wash.
- Deliver the local newspaper to houses in your area and get paid to exercise.
- Install solar panels and start saving on your electricity.
- Only use your credit card for Internet purchases and lower your credit card limit; make it a priority to wipe out your outstanding balance every month.

Practical Wealth Creation

We are now going to go into more detail on how to build wealth and protect it. First, write down your plan in accordance with your age.

If a Young Person

- You want to finish your diploma/degree or three-year apprenticeship.
- Prepare to live at home and save before you get married.
- At the end of your diploma/degree, you may reassess the use of your money and buy a car or save towards a home deposit.

If Married with Young Children

- Make extra payments on your mortgage to drastically cut down the interest.
- Buy an investment property, or top up your superannuation.
- Plan to retire by age sixty.

If a Retired Couple

- Make sure you have a will in place.
- Apply for any pension benefits; it all helps.

Key point: Your superannuation should only complement your investment. The average superannuation only lasts about five years when you are retired. Also, focus on investment terms, not only on the tax benefits. Taxes should not drive your decisions.

In protecting your assets, only buy as little insurance as you need. Get independent advice; insurance agents will generally sell you more than you need, as they are paid by commission.

Key point: A budget is not a rigid document designed to make your life miserable. It's a flexible tool to make your life better. As I mentioned before, it is highly beneficial to do a spreadsheet of your expenses. Each time you pay for something, write it down; for example, write down your bank, credit union, and credit card payments under the heading on your spreadsheet.

Note: Draw cash out to cover all those small things that you don't record in your spreadsheet. Put the cash amount withdrawn into your cash column.

For example: Spreadsheet page 1

Date	Housekeeping	Home Maintenance	Books and DVDs	Health Care	Take-aways	Internet	Mobile

Spreadsheet page 2

Date	Gas	Electricity	Accountant	Cash	Garden	Investment Property	Social	Vitamin Supplements

Spreadsheet 3

Date	Shoes and Clothes	Car Costs	Land Rate	Water Rates	Charity	Home Insurance	Holidays	Miscellaneous

2016 Home Cash Flow

Saturday date	Week #	Income	Total	Expenses	Total	Total Change	Average per week

Investment Property Cash Flow 2016

Saturday date	Week #	Income	Total	Expenses	Total	Total Change	Average per week

Remember to pay yourself 10 percent first and put that into a separate high-yielding online account (or if you are more self-disciplined, into your offset account, which is tax sheltered). That is, you save interest but do not have to declare it on your tax return and be taxed at your marginal rate. If your company had to reduce your income by 10 percent, you could adjust your lifestyle spending habits, and you would make it.

The Rule of 72

Use the rule of 72 as a guide to show you how long your savings and investment would take to double in value based on compound interest. It is very effective and easy to use. Here are some examples:

• Property increasing at 10 percent per annum:

For example, 72 ÷ 10 = 7.2 years to double

You divide the increase into 72, and that is how long your property would take to double in value.

For example, 72 ÷ 6 = 12 years to double, so if your property averaged 6 percent per annum, it would take twelve years to double.

For example, 72 ÷ 15 = 4.8 years; if your property had a building boom period averaging 15 percent per annum, it would take 4.8 years to double in value.

Let's say you put your money into the bank and got 3 percent per annum; for example, 72 ÷ 3 = 24; that means it would take twenty-four years to double in value.

There are banks in Europe that are now only offering minus 0.5 percent; in other words, they are charging you to keep your money. In that case, people would be better off to keep their cash at home.

Key point: It takes time for the magic of compound interest to show results; it starts slowly and then really jumps, so the earlier you start, the better.

Tips to Help You Save

Don't say, "I am only going window shopping for fun," or you will end up buying things you don't need with money you don't have.

Here is a tough one: Don't buy something unless you have the money to pay for it.

Whenever possible, pay with cash; don't use credit card.

If you must use your credit card, make sure you are in a position to pay the monthly balance outright.

Here is an interesting fact regarding credit cards: The February 2007 reserve bank figures show we each spend around $14,300 on our credit cards each year. The average outstanding debt is $2,800 per card (and many people have more than one card). The banks make more money when you have a lot of credit cards; the interest-free period only starts with a zero balance. Many people choose to pay the minimum monthly amount and roll the bulk of the account into the next billing period. This may seem easy on your hip pocket, but you are actually compounding your debt and are heading towards bankruptcy. You have to kill that card before it kills you. Let's say you book a holiday costing $2,000 with a credit card that has 15 percent rate per annum, and you choose to pay the minimum 2 percent. It will take you 264 months (twenty-two years) to pay it off. The interest would have been $2,790, assuming you had no additional purchases; the majority of people live like this.

Also, be aware of interest-free financing. What is not pointed out is, if the item is not paid off in full during the interest-free period, interest will be charged at exorbitant rates on the outstanding balance. Now interest-free finance with a free credit card is a real trap for the uninformed. If you make additional purchases on these credit cards, you will be immediately charged with interest of around 27 percent. Cut these cards up before they cut you up.

When it comes to personal loans, always try to get funds from a bank building society or credit union, as their rates will be significantly lower than a finance company; loans for second-hand cars often attract a higher rate than loans for new cars. However, remember a new car is going to take a big hit in the first year with depreciation. Also, be careful if you take out a secured loan against a home just to get a lower rate, as you could lose the roof over your head if you are unable to make the repayments.

Do not borrow and add it to your mortgage. Let's say you wanted $10,000 for an overseas holiday and thought you would add it to your mortgage because of lower rates than a personal loan. The big problem with that is, the length of the loan is usually ten times longer. If you had a $300,000 twenty-five-year loan at 7.5 percent interest rate (average for life of the loan), your $10,000 holiday would cost you $11,700 in interest, plus you would have to pay back the original $10,000. The total cost of your holiday would be $21,700. Bottom line: Never add any other loan to your mortgage. The saying "It's on the house" (free) is the exact opposite of what you would experience. The only one that profits is the bank; you are now contributing to their excessively fat profits.

Actually, there are different kinds of debt: debt that helps and debt that hurts. The worst kind is disastrous debt. It is using high-interest credit cards to buy things that don't last, such as entertainment and holidays. I am personally not against you having fun, but don't use high interest to get that fleeting euphoria. The next is unfortunately necessary debt, like buying a car; sadly, most of us cannot pay cash. A car will fall in value and cost you money to run, but to have some flexibility in life, it is necessary. Then there is happily necessary debt; this would be your own home, to give you stability and an asset which will increase in value. Finally, there is effective debt, like negative gearing. This asset, like an investment home, grows in value, plus you have the tax deductions to help your cash flow. You must be emotionally and financially prepared with the knowledge that your tenants can get behind in their payments (our tenants have from time to time), and house prices can fall at the wrong time in your life.

Do not ever borrow money to buy shares; the share market is very volatile. Also, the world share market is distorted by quantitative easing (money printed by the Federal Reserve); this distorts the basic rules of capitalism. The moment your collateral value goes down (e.g., share value), the banks put a margin call on you (i.e., they ask for some of your money) and you have to sell shares, often at a loss.

The bottom line is, do not take on more debt than you can comfortably manage. When it comes to a long-term debt like a home mortgage, factor in possible interest rate rises to see if you could meet the extra payments. Remember, agreeing to take on more credit is an easy way to bury yourself in debt; remember what I have said already: Do not make tax deductibility the main reason for your investment. Also, unless you are sticking to a budget, you could simply end up accumulating more debt again.

If you want to consolidate all your debts with one loan, you need to know whether you can meet the new payments comfortably. A good rule of thumb is your monthly debt repayments should not exceed 33 percent of your gross monthly income. Always keep in the back of your mind, if the balance of your home loan rises above 80 percent of the value of your home, your lender will ask you to take out mortgage insurance. A lot of people think that this protects you. No, it protects the lender.

Bottom line: Debt consolidation can be an effective strategy but will only work if you break the spending habits that got you into debt in the first place. Why do most people succeed with their mortgages? Because the lender carries a big stick: If you don't pay your mortgage, they simply take back the house. You do get aberrations in the property market; it is not an even 7.2 percent compound interest (that is the average increase in value over the last thirty years). For example, in 1994, a Sydney home cost $193,000. In 2005, a Sydney home cost $495,000.

Note: Perth's medium house price was $495,000 in April 2016. Some pundits say to rent and invest the difference from the cost of paying off the home mortgage, including land rates and so on. The reality is, very few invest the difference; they spend the difference. My concern for people who rent and spend the difference is that in retirement, they end up with no home and no money. The benefit, of course, in staying with the mortgage (even through the tough times) is that one day, the mortgage will come to an end, and you will own your own home. Renting may well go on forever.

However, if you sell your home every eight years or less, then renting may prove to be a better proposition. Frequent buying and selling generates excessive costs, including stamp duties, legal fees, removal costs, and agent's fees (up to 6 percent of the purchase price). The bottom line is, if you buy in a good location at a fair price and hold for the long term, owning a home debt-free remains a very sensible goal and a cornerstone of wealth. Merilyn and I belong to a property club, which does the research for us. It has saved us a lot of time and money and worry.

The cost of moving from one house to the other is really quite staggering. Let's look at moving from a two-bedroom $300,000 house to a four-bedroom $540,000 house in 2015:

- Agent's fees: 2.5 percent (negotiable) $13,500
- stamp duty: $17,650

- solicitor's fees: $2,000
- removal van charges: $2,000
- building and pest inspections: $500
- search and surveys: $330
- electricity and phone connections: $300
- other insurances: $500
- Total $36,950

The bottom line with mortgages is that you must shop around and play one lender against the other; remember, they are fighting for market share, and they need your business. I mentioned you must factor in rate increases. Over the long term, it is inevitable that rates will rise. I had a mortgage in June 1989; the major banks were charging 17 percent. On a $150,000 mortgage over twenty-five years, the monthly repayment was $2,150 per month. Just think, if that happened again on a $300,000 mortgage, your payment would be $4,300 per month. If you feel you could not possibly afford any more, then fix or partly fix your mortgage: 50 percent fixed and 50 percent variable, especially in this low-interest environment (as of April 2016, banks have just reduced interest rates 0.25 percent). These rates are at historically low levels; there will probably be more rate reductions of 0.25 percent, but that leaves a lot of room for upward rate increases too.

Some people do not understand what and how effective a mortgage offset account is. Here it is in a nutshell:

Say you had a $400,000 loan, and you put $30,000 of your savings into an offset account; the lender will only charge you interest on ($400,000 - $30,000) = $370,000. If your mortgage rate over the next ten years climbed to 7.5 percent, you have saved ($30,000 × 7.5%) = $2,250 per annum.

If you had put that into a savings account, say, getting you 5 percent in ten years' time, your savings would be $30,000 × 5% = $1,500.

However, you have to declare this $1,500 on your tax return, and if your marginal rate of tax was 32.5 percent, you would lose $1,500 × 32.2% = $487.50, so your net savings result would be $1,500 - $487.50 = $1,012.50.

So you would have only received less than 50 percent from a savings account compared to an offset account. You actually ate your cake and had it, as you still have daily access to your offset account and online banking; you can pay bills from it. Now your most effective strategy is this: Pay all your bills by credit card, transfer your pay into your offset account, and at the end of the month, pay out your end-of-month credit card balance in full, and so pay no interest. Yet your money has been reducing your daily interest amount.

A very effective strategy to shorten your mortgage is to simply make additional payments. The amount comes straight off the principal. For example, an extra $10 per week on a $200,000 mortgage at 7.25 percent interest, over twenty-five years, can cut out two years of payments and save $21,000 in interest. Another way to cut years off your loan is to pay half your monthly repayment every fortnight. It is effective because you end up paying thirteen monthly instalments per year and not twelve.

Lump-sum payments (say, on your tax return) are very effective. Let's say you put $2,400 towards your $300,000 twenty-five year 7.25 percent loan; at the end of the first year, your interest would have been reduced by nearly $12,000 and shaved one year off the mortgage. If you could make extra payments of $20 per week, together with a lump sum payment, you would boost the interest saved to $40,000 and be mortgage-free five years sooner. It is the magic of compound interest in reverse.

The next effective key would be to go for a shorter term. Let's say you were offered a $200,000 mortgage for twenty-five years at 7 percent; you would pay more than $224,000 in interest. If you made the loan over fifteen years, although your monthly payments would rise almost $400 per month, you would save nearly $100,000 in interest.

Superannuation should complement property investment, not replace it. It has a favourable tax treatment. Pretax contributions are only taxed at 15 percent, the same as the investment earnings. Once you are over sixty, you can take it all out, tax free.

As I said before, people don't plan to fail; they fail to plan. You must plan now so you can retire with dignity and be in a financial position to help the less fortunate. Here is a sobering statistic: Today, there are 2.6 million Australians aged sixty-five or more (13 percent of the population). By 2040, that figure will double. Pensions account for 30 percent of the government Social Security budget, and it is already under a strain. The only recourse the government has in the future is to greatly increase taxes or extend the age limit and increase the assets and income test, making it harder to qualify.

In 2007, there were five people in the workforce for every person in retirement. By 2040, there will be fewer than three people working for every retired person. The bottom line: As I mentioned before, if you don't save, you don't invest, and if you don't invest, you will have nothing (apart from your home, if you have one) to retire on. The Australian people unfortunately are not good savers; they are amongst the worst in the world. Since 2002, we have had a negative savings rate; in 2005, we reached an all-time low of -3 percent (down from +19 percent in the late 1970s). If you cannot afford it, then do not buy it or pay cash, like our earlier generation did.

Research has shown that the 9.5 percent superannuation guaranteed (compulsory superannuation) is not nearly enough for you to live on in retirement. If you saved 15 percent of your income from age twenty, you would be able to retire on about 75 percent of your final salary at age sixty-five.

What is salary sacrifice? It is simply asking your employer to pay into your superannuation account before you pay income tax. If you are on the top rate of 45 cents in the dollar, you have only 55 cents per dollar left on income that falls into that top margin. If you salary sacrifice (that is, reduce your salary and put it into superannuation), you only pay 15 cents contributions tax (not income tax rates) and have 85 cents in the dollar left flowing into your superannuation. Then at age sixty, you can take out that 85 cents in the dollar, plus all the accumulated interest, and that total amount is tax free. Salary sacrifice really helps the person who is paying the top income tax rate.

Say you earn $80,000 per annum and are fifty years of age, and your children have left home; if you put $300 per week (that is, your employer agreed to reduce your salary by $300 per week and put it straight into your superannuation account), your final balance would go from $150,400 to $312,600 at age sixty.

Now coming back to the investment property, the home that you live in is not subject to capital gains tax; only your investment property is. It is quite generous; it is simply your profit less genuine expenses (mortgage, land rates, etc.) divided by two times your marginal rate of tax. For example, your marginal tax rate is 30 percent, your profit was $150,000, so your tax would be 150,000 ÷ 2 = $75,000 × 30% = $22,500, so you would pocket ($150,000 - $22,500) = $127,500.

We hear a lot about negative gearing; for those who are not familiar with this strategy, gearing simply means borrowing money to invest. The main draw is that you claim the interest you pay as a tax deduction. The bottom line is, make sure the investment you are putting borrowed money towards is sound; that is why I recommend property for your negative gearing.

Choose the Lowest Tax Bracket for Savings

This is a very effective way for couples to reduce their total amount of tax. You simply put your investment in the person's name with the lower tax rate. The first $18,000 is tax free (it used to be only $6,000). Let's say one of the couple was earning $20,000 per annum; they would only pay tax on the lowest marginal rate. Although you cannot split income from wages, you can certainly put your savings with the one in the lowest marginal rate of tax. Although there are a lot of tax agents around, I highly recommend a qualified accountant. They more than pay for their fees, which is also a tax deduction for the next financial year. When you receive your tax refund, put it straight into your offset account before you are tempted to spend it.

The cardinal rule of investment is, do not get into something you don't understand. The anxiety it usually causes is not worth the monetary gain. When it comes to investing in shares, the fundamentals have been skewed by quantitative easing in the United States, which affects other markets (we are inextricably linked in this world economy). If you are not professionally trained, keep away from them. I have talked with many friends who tried online share trading, and few of them have made money. Taking excessive risks and looking for big returns is the number one reason why investors lose their money. A good truism is "Don't put all your eggs in one basket." In other words, diversify. Don't try and outguess the market in trying to buy low and sell high. Most people lose (unless they have divine intervention by the Holy Spirit).

Let's look at property in more detail. Australia has 7.6 million households; around 2.2 million are rentals. Property has historically doubled every ten years; that is, 7.2 percent per annum compound interest. Try to buy an investment property that has the following, or join a property club who will do the research for you (it is the best thing Merilyn and I did):

- is close to city centre

- is close to amenities, schools, and shops
- is where future infrastructure will increase in value
- is pleasant to the eye

Forward Planning

As a guideline, buying costs are about 4.5 percent of the purchasing price. Selling costs are about 3.1 percent of the selling price, and cash flow is extremely important. Ask yourself, can you cover negative cash flow for the first two to four years? We use the property club founded by Kevin Young, Australia's most successful property club. This organisation has created more millionaires than anyone else. He was a millionaire at twenty-seven and has gladly passed on his wealth of experience (no pun intended).

In your future predicted cash flow, always factor in inflation. Depending on how many years it takes to get you to a positive cash flow on your rental property, you can then work out if you have enough income or reserve money to pay for all the associated costs in keeping a property. You have to decide whether you are going to manage the rental property yourself. My rental property is in Brisbane, and I live in Perth, so it was a no-brainer to have a property manager. Think about it: Even if it is in your home state, are you prepared to chase up the rent if it is late or go before the residential tenancy tribunal in the event of a dispute? I have had to claim on our landlord's rent insurance, and the property manager has been excellent in arranging any repairs, chasing up late rent, and informing us of any problems and handling them for us.

The next thing is whether you decide to start a business. There are success stories where many started with stock in their garage. Some have started with a bricks-and-mortar retail business; however, the overhead is crippling, and many find that working seventy hour weeks is common, and it can take five years just to break even.

You may be interested to know that by June 2014, there were 2,121,235 operators of small businesses in Australia; 51.6 percent of these are home-based businesses (that is, 1,094,557). Be careful trying a physical bricks-and-mortar retail business. Dick Smith, an icon in Australian business, went bust, and Walmart recently closed 139 stores in America because they cannot compete with Internet businesses.

This now brings us to franchising. There were approximately 1,160 franchisors who sold 79,000 franchises, an increase of 8.2 percent in 2012–2014. This suits people with little or no business experience. They vary from the very well-known MacDonald's, Pizza Hut, and KFC down to carpet cleaning, lawn mowing, pet grooming, and real estate businesses. The purchase price can range from a low of $6,000 to in excess of $1,000,000. The major cost is royalty payments, which can range from 7 to 12 percent of your gross income. Independent research from Edith Cowan University in Western Australia found that franchises are 2.5 times less likely to fail than small independent businesses. Yes, you certainly pay for the name and the business formula.

Retirement

Most of those aged over sixty-five receive a pension; the bottom line, especially for young readers of this book, is to start putting away into superannuation from the day you start work. You need more than the compulsory superannuation. The 2014 federal budget deferred the superannuation guaranteed (SG) rate of three years, so the rate will remain at 9.5 percent for seven years, until 2021, and then increase by 0.5 percent each following year, until the SG reaches 12 percent in July 2025. Eighteen-year-olds would need to put aside 12 percent of their salary to retire on 75 percent of their final salary. However, at age thirty-five, the contribution needs to be 30 percent of their final salary, and at age forty-five, their contribution would need to be 49 percent of their final salary, so they can retire on 75 percent of their final salary.

The age pension benefits as of May, 2016 include energy supplements as follows:

A single pension is $873.90 per fortnight

A combined pension is $1,317.40 per fortnight.

So you can see it is essential that you have no mortgage and a reasonable superannuation pay-out to complement your age pension.

We are now going to look at financial freedom from the word of God and get a biblical perspective on this interesting and important subject which affects all of us; this is especially true when we look at the lifestyle of Americans.

Debt has become a way of life in America. I am sorry to say that the church has also adopted this lifestyle. Most people are employed in jobs they dislike because they are boxed in by debt payments and responsibilities. The Bible says, "Godliness with contentment is great gain." Jesus said in Mark 4 that "the deceitfulness of riches chokes out the word of God." Many people think they would be happy if they could just get the things they want. It is true that things can be a blessing, but true happiness comes from who we are in Christ and not what we possess.

As I mentioned in the section on the global financial system, America's government has a $19.9 trillion debt. To give you an idea, if you spent $100 per second, it would take you 316.8 years to spend that much. This will never be repaid. American families are in a situation proportional to the government's dire financial state. The public uses thirty-year mortgages to finance their homes and seven-year loans to finance their cars. You can see that because of the quick availability of financing, the national work ethic and the worth of the dollar have both been devalued in America (the same applies to Australia, but to a lesser extent). Retailers know more people will pay their asking price if they can pay it off; this utilisation of debt drives prices higher. The American government, like many others in the Western world, has a progressive tax structure, which penalises those who become successful through hard work. So why do people go into debt so readily? Debt gives people all the things that success offers, without requiring them to pay the price to succeed. Debt allows anyone to experience prosperity for a season, but eventually, the truth will come out. I am sure you have heard about many professional athletes who have made millions but ended up broke; many lottery winners go broke after just a few years.

When I was an investment consultant with Westpac, I met with many hundreds of families, and the sad truth is, it did not matter what their income or profession was. Most were severely in debt and were far closer to financial trouble than they realised. Through my research, I found this to be the same for American families. "We buy things we don't need, with money we don't have, to impress people we don't know." The bottom line is, the result of discontentment, such as stress, hopelessness and rebellion against God, are a few of the problems that surface from serving money.

I hope now after reading part 1 that you realise we are no longer under the Old Covenant system. When we decided to pray, and give as we were led by the Holy Spirit, God gave us strategies to get out of debt. It is such a wonderful feeling to have retired three years ago, and still be able to help my friends and give to charities and to Christian evangelism and to missionary work.

I read that only 21 percent of Americans have actually paid off their homes; also, 36 percent of Americans do not have anything saved for their retirement, and 35 percent of Americans over sixty-five rely completely on Social Security.

Here is a wonderful promise from God:

"Be anxious for nothing, but in everything by prayer and supplication, with thanksgiving, let your requests be made known to God;

and the peace of God, which surpasses all understanding, will guard your hearts and minds through Christ Jesus" (Philippians 4:6–7 NKJV).

The bottom line is, I present my needs to God in prayer with thanksgiving because I know He cares for me, and He will honour His word. The peace of God is mine because I know that the thing that I have put before Him is done, even though I see no change. If I didn't believe it was done, I would still be anxious.

Faith is the currency of the New Kingdom:

"Now faith is the substance of things hoped for, the evidence of things not seen" (Hebrews 11:1 NKJV).

This may shock some people, but God is not moved by need alone; otherwise, the greatest move in providing for people's needs would be in India and Africa. In the early days, I did not understand why God did not solve my financial needs. He couldn't do much until I had faith, for it changed my spending habits and moved from Old Covenant formulas to a New Covenant relationship with Jesus Christ. Make a commitment from today not to use debt as a way of life but to wait on the Lord for direction. Base your life on His kingdom principles, and you will win.

Key point: The only heaven you will experience is the heaven you grasp by faith and release into your life. When the Apostle Paul needed help financially, the church gave him a gift, and Paul was letting them do it. By giving into the kingdom, they had a right to withdraw from the kingdom to get their needs met. Philippians 4:19

(NKJV) is a response to their giving: "And my God shall supply all your need according to His riches in glory by Christ Jesus."

The core of the problem is lust for things and the pride of life, which are spiritual things that must be dealt with. We don't deal with diseased leaves, we deal with the roots of the tree; if we don't eradicate the underlying cause, debt will again return to you and your family.

Wealth

Let's look at the twelve consequences of wealth and what they mean to you:

1. Wealth Is Relative

Wherever money is concerned, we tend to measure ourselves against someone who has much more rather than someone who has much less.

We need to measure ourselves against the suffering and afflicted, realising that against that situation, we are rich, and that is why wealth is relative.

2. Wealth Is Commitment

Study and prepare and look for your opportunity.

Only the rich can help the poor; you cannot help the poor if you are one yourself.

3. Wealth Is Responsibility

Provide people a place to live (that is, an investment property).

4. Wealth Is Accountability

Study and increase in knowledge so you are more valuable to your employer.

Exercise so you will have more stamina for your occupation.

Eat nutritiously so you will have better health and no sick days.

Get direction from God. He will teach you how to profit and lead the way that you should go.

Isaiah 48:17 (NKJV) says, "Thus says the LORD, your Redeemer, the Holy One of Israel: 'I am the LORD your God, who teaches you to profit, who leads you by the way you should go.'"

5. Wealth Is Leadership

Show people how to prosper so they in turn can help others.

6. Wealth Is Power

God almighty is happy to give you the power to get wealth so you can establish His covenant, the kingdom of God, on this earth.

Ecclesiastes 2:26 (NKJV) says, "For God gives wisdom and knowledge and joy to a man who is good in His sight; but to the sinner He gives the work of gathering and collecting, that he may give to him who is good before God. This also is vanity and grasping for the wind."

7. Wealth Is Giving

I have never heard any reports of money falling from heaven in answer to prayer, but I have heard of people giving their wealth in response to prayer.

8. Wealth Is Influence

Your word carries more weight when it is backed up by some wealth; it also opens up doors that a poor man would not have access to.

9. Wealth Is Pressure

Many would not even think that wealth is pressure. Please consider: You have to guard it, keep from losing it, and be a good steward of it. To whom much is given, much is required.

10. Wealth Is Sacrifice

Wealth requires study and planning, combined with action and timing.

11. Wealth Brings Criticism

Two things are certain: Everyone pays tax, and everyone dies, but the wealthy have continuous criticism. Remember: Criticism is the greatest tool for those who do not get involved; why? It builds them up and pulls down the victim.

Key point: Try to ignore criticism. Why? Judge not, unless you want to be judged; besides, there are no statues for critics.

12. Wealth Is Courage

In 1992, during the Australian recession, my life insurance clients started to stop paying their premiums. Their policies lapsed, and under the agency agreements, I had to pay back the commissions. I was overwhelmed and had to sell my family home in Perth and start all over again. In 1998, I was introduced to the teachings of Gary Carpenter (that was in the days of cassette tapes). He was praying four hours per day in tongues and eventually started writing down faith and grace teachings. His foundational scripture for all New Covenant Christians was 2 Corinthians 8:9 (NKJV): "For you know the grace of our Lord Jesus Christ, that though He was rich, yet for your sakes He became poor, that you through His poverty might become rich."

The person who wants above-average wealth has to be prepared to take an above-average risk. The New Covenant advocates giving as one of the keys to receiving more than enough for your personal needs.

Luke 6:38 (NKJV) says, "Give, and it will be given to you: good measure, pressed down, shaken together, and running over will be put into your bosom. For with the same measure that you use, it will be measured back to you."

There are two broad types of people: There are pensioners who have time but not enough money, and there are business people who have money but not enough time. A third category that is now developing (and more prevalent than twenty years ago) is property investors. Through tax deductions, rental income, and property growth value, they are able to make a small sacrifice in cash flow and consequently have a more comfortable and satisfying life in their later years. When you sacrifice, you are in good company; the greatest sacrifice was made two thousand years ago, and mankind has been benefiting from it ever since.

A final thought is worth repeating: Whatever God tells you to do, do it. If you have to have a formula, there it is. I am so thankful that this has worked out so well for Merilyn and me and our close friends who have embraced this wonderful, liberating way of the New Covenant when it comes to physical, emotional, and spiritual prosperity.

PART 5

Excellent Health

What is the point of achieving this wealth-creation plan if you have poor health and are unable to enjoy it? I have helped many people through my work; some of these people were in poor health and said they would gladly swap most of their money if they could just be well and enjoy life again. Looking back, it seems crazy to spend all of your time getting wealth, only to find you have to spend much of it trying to regain your health.

New diseases and conditions are always being identified. Many of them are developing because of the increased stress, which is due to the complex, fast-paced modern world and the poor-quality processed food we are putting into our bodies.

Here are some interesting facts:

- In one year, Westerners consume three pounds of chemicals from our foods.
- The worst hazard is the consumption of sugar.
- Consumption of sugar has gone from 3 pounds per annum in 1850 to 150 pounds per annum in 2010.
- One great cause which accounts for the majority of cases of longevity is eating in moderation and the quality of food.

- Thirty minutes of exercise per day, four times a week will improve your metabolism.
- You can have stress without distress; it depends on how you handle it.
- Sugar increases blood viscosity and is a prime factor of triggering off a heart attack.
- You are as old as your arteries.
- Your arteries are as old as you make them.
- A blood pressure reading of 120 over 80 is a good reading. The "120" is systolic and it equals the pressure put out by the heart. The "80" is diastolic and is the pressure between beats coming back into the heart.

Key point: The purity of your blood determines your mental and physical state.

Social Stress Scale

1. Death of spouse = 100 points
2. Divorce = 73 points
3. Marital separation = 65 points
4. Jail = 63 points
5. Death in the family = 63 points
6. Illness = 53 points
7. Job dismissal = 47 points
8. Retirement = 45 points
9. Christmas = 12 points

Note: 150 points = 51 percent illness

Summary on Cholesterol

Natural body cholesterol is high-density lipoproteins (HDL); this is an essential fat. It provides stability in every cell of your body.

Egg yolks are extremely high in fat. They contain about 68 percent of our allowed daily intake. The egg white contains a lot of essential nutrients; eggs have an important place in our diet.

The most unfavourable method to reduce cholesterol is by drugs, which reduces natural cholesterol.

Eating sugar and drinking alcohol and smoking cigarettes reduces the good cholesterol HDL.

The only foods that contain cholesterol are meat, fish, eggs, sardines, chicken, shellfish, dairy products, and eggs.

Social and Economic Cost

In America, physicians perform over four hundred thousand bypass operations and place over one million stents in clogged arteries per year. Tragically, 2,200 Americans die each day of cardiovascular disease, and coronary heart disease claims one in every six deaths. In the United States, $2.5 trillion was spent on health care last year. That is a staggering 16 percent of America's gross domestic product (that is, the turnover of all goods and services). The disconcerting fact, though, is despite the vast sum of money spent, the United States is ranked thirty-seventh in the world in health outcomes.

North America consumes 47.7 percent of all the pharmaceuticals made in the entire world; its population is 4.3 percent of the world. The bottom line is, Western medicine focuses on disease without getting to the underlying cause, and physicians are trained to offer a drug or surgical procedure.

Offering medication without including instructions on how to reverse the disease process is short-sighted. Treating disease after it occurs is not the solution. Western medicine is great for acute care, say, if you are having a heart attack or if you have just been involved in an accident.

Conventional medicine falls short in prevention and chronic disease care. It is ill to the pill, not long-term prevention.

Now, human beings are triune beings, that is spirit, soul (mind, will, and emotions), and body. Holistic treatment would be treating all three, not just ill to the pill, which is treating the symptoms and not the underlying cause. Holistic doctors promote wellness and treat patients using preventative integrated medicine. This is a more desirable approach, so the human body will not build up a resistance towards antibiotics and other medicines.

The word of God teaches that happiness is like good medicine. In fact, all people have the ability to heal; we need to tap into the body's innate power. It is very hard to do this if we are stressed out because stress supresses our immune system. Love is the most powerful healer. One of the most important things that physicians can do for their patient is to treat every individual with kindness, acceptance, and grace, not judgement.

You Are More than Your Genes

There is overwhelming evidence by numerous studies that there are incredibly strong links between chronic stress and poor health. Stress is a recognised risk factor for a number of diseases, including heart disease, diabetes, and high blood pressure. A recent research paper on high-stressed women showed that they had a cell age of ten years older than their biological age.

Research has shown that with the right food, you do not need medicine. I am sixty-seven and not on medicine. We have an aquaponics system where we grow our own food in the backyard. There are edible fish in a one thousand-litre tank and a grow bed over it, connected by a pump and hose that transports the fish emulsion to feed the vegetables. The emulsion gets caught on the roots of the vegetables, and the clean water is returned via a pipe into the fish tank. So the fish always have clean water, the vegetables are continually watered and fertilised, and we get to eat lovely fresh vegetables and fish.

The right foods send a signal to our genes to produce a protein that prevents heart disease, Alzheimer's disease, arthritis, and inflammation. Foods that are high in white refined flour and sugar send a signal to our genes to produce proteins that result in arthritis, back pain, shoulder pain, heart disease, and memory loss. What we eat really matters.

Further research by cardiologists in the United States has shown a high-fat meal keeps the blood vessel from dilating for as long as six hours. A diet with large quantities of saturated fats (a diet of beef, pork, or lamb, for example) results in diminished blood flow to the heart.

Also found repeatedly is that red meat, processed meat, and cured meat are linked to colon cancer. Another fact that came out was there were a hundred thousand deaths per annum from cancer that were related to being overweight and having too much sugar and simple carbohydrates in the diet. Diving through the archives of medicine showed that those who took fruit and vegetables, particularly those who took green leafy vegetables, were protected against heart disease and stroke. Many people do not know that green leafy vegetables are high in calcium and magnesium (which releases nutrients into the muscles) and are very low in sugar.

Studies have shown that older people, seventy to ninety years of age, who follow a Mediterranean diet and simply walk 1.5 kilometres per day have a 50 percent lower incident of cardiac events.

Note: The Mediterranean diet focuses on healthy fats, fruits and vegetables. People have also been shown to reduce cancer and extend their life by eating beans, lentils, legumes, whole foods, fruit and fish. True prosperity definitely includes quality of life and not just quantity of life. They are encouraged (even told) to stay away from saturated fats, such as pork, lamb, cream, and butter, but eat a lot of omega 3s, which are polyunsaturated.

It is well worth taking omega 3 supplements or eating more fish. This sends a signal to your genes to produce proteins that prevent blood from clotting and block inflammation, which is linked to heart disease, Alzheimer's, and arthritis. This is one of the key ingredients of the Mediterranean diet's success. When I was consulting in the work force, I met a man in Perth whose brother died of a heart attack at age fifty-nine. An examination by the doctor showed his arteries were clogged with LDL cholesterol (remember: L = lousy). This gave his brother a warning to look after his own life, so he changed his doctor, and his new doctor told him to start eating much more fish and to take omega 3 supplements. Apply this golden rule to your dinner plate. Fill half your plate with green leafy vegetables, including broccoli and asparagus. Fill one quarter of your plate with brown rice, beans, and lentils. Another quarter of that includes good fats (HDL cholesterol; H = happy) like olive oil, wild salmon, and omega 3 powerhouse foods.

Aim for nutritional super plants: foods that are not processed, refined, or filtered. Whole foods are very high in photo nutrients, which mainly come from plants, vegetables, and fruits. It has been shown that whole foods provide far greater vitamins and minerals than we get from processed food.

These photo nutrients can boost the immune system and prevent cancer. They are anti-inflammatory and can prevent heart disease and Alzheimer's disease. The deeper the colour of the food (the darker the berry or the grape), the more photo nutrients it contains. So vegetables, fruits, nuts, and olive oil are excellent sources of photo nutrients.

What I am about to say is different from our eating habits and our culture. Research has shown that when food is consumed more frequently, but in smaller amounts (that is, frequent snacks instead of three full meals), the level of blood sugar (glucose) remains steady.

Food Allergies

People who constantly react unfavourably to a dietary substance are said to be allergic to it. Correcting one's diet automatically eliminates many allergies because the most common allergies are foods that should be avoided by everybody anyway. The most common allergies occur because of a confused response by the white blood cells, due to a built-in immune system defect, originating from wrong feeding as an infant. Nature intended infants to be breastfed. A baby's digestive system cannot properly cope with any other kind of food; mother's milk not only provides perfect nutrition for the child, it provides immunological substances to protect against infection, until the child's own immune system is completely developed.

Here are some key points to improve digestion, which is a key to treating allergies naturally:

- Eat only when hungry.
- Do not eat when tired or under stress.
- Eat in a tranquil atmosphere.
- Eat slowly and chew food well.
- Eat smaller, more frequent meals.
- Don't drink alcohol with meals.

These foods cause most allergies: cow's milk, wheat, corn, and eggs.

Key point: Research has shown that compared to the poorer populations in the world, civilised people consume up to seven times as much fat, six times as much sugar, and double the protein. It has been shown that native civilisations on very low-fat, low-cholesterol diets do not show signs of heart disease or diabetes.

Here is a revealing experiment: A study of effects on rats and mice comparing processed food with natural food showed that the animals on the natural diet remained sleek and healthy. The processed food group were nervous and bit the people handling them, and many of them grew to twice the size in girth. Later, all the mice were given an unrestricted choice of both diets, and the researchers were surprised when all the mice showed preference to the processed foods, and they ate twice as much as the other group. The healthy mice subsequently took on the appearance of the processed food mice after they were fed the same food and soon developed skin diseases like the others, which shows that processed foods are made to taste nice but are not good for you.

Food Addiction

Most people are concerned with the degree of alcoholism and drug addiction that has caused so much misery and death, but there is also a national addiction caused by Western food. It is ironic that many people who are appalled by drugs and alcohol could be classified as food-a-holics, and many such people end up as chronic invalids and are just as much a burden to society as alcoholics.

Weight control is really fat control; just remember that being slim doesn't mean you have clear arteries. The key is you have to cut down calories and increase energy output. Simply eat less and move more. The reason that so many slimming diets fail in the long term is that most people find them unsatisfying and abandon them, sooner or later. The bottom line is, people who cannot break their addiction to rich food will always have a weight problem. The important thing about any diet is that it must contain all the essential nutrients.

It has been shown that a low-fat vegetarian diet, preferably uncooked, achieves all the benefits of fasting, but without depriving the body of any essential vitamins and minerals. This diet covers all the aspects of optimum health and is also slimming.

Simple refined carbohydrates are like dynamite. They are high in calories, and by causing hypoglycaemia, they induce hunger and therefore cause you to eat more. Candy, for example, contains by weight six times the calories of boiled potatoes and eight times that of apples, but it is completely devoid of any nutritional value. No wonder sugar is named "white death" and "sweet poison"; we will look at that in greater depth later on.

It is not surprising that all alcohol, including beer, is a refined carbohydrate. However, on the other hand, natural complex carbohydrates are not only nourishing but are filling too. Complex carbohydrates contain only half the calories as its equivalent of fat. Most slimming diets are high in protein and low in carbohydrates, mainly because carbohydrates are considered a villain, but this is quite wrong.

Key point: If you ate nothing except complex carbohydrate food consisting of a reasonable variation of cereals, fruit, and vegetables, your body would receive the ideal energy food. The benefit is you would always satisfy your appetite without eating enough calories to make you fat.

Research has shown also that a low-fat, low-protein, high-complex-carbohydrate diet gives protection against all degenerative diseases at the same time. People who change to a low-fat vegetarian diet are invariably lean and healthy; they lose the desire for tasty things that had originally done them so much harm.

Remember that exercise is an important but secondary factor in weight control. Fat has no food value, and therefore the body has no use for it; it will be stored in your body as fat and will be very hard to remove. That is why you see so many determined but unsuccessful overweight joggers; unless they change their diet and cut right down on fat and alcohol, they will always remain over weight.

Definition of Fitness

Fitness is the condition of the body (and mind) which enables it to perform its assignments efficiently, without undue strain or fatigue, with adequate reserves.

Ways to obtain physical fitness include long vigorous walks, jogging, distance cycling, distance swimming, or other such endurance exercise, done preferably daily for the best results. It should be carefully graduated initially because not only may the heart overload, you have to give time for ankles and knees to be strengthened.

Disclaimer – Check with your doctor before starting an exercise program.

A good way to check your heart recovery is as follows:

- After the exercise, sit and rest for one minute.
- Take your pulse rate over thirty seconds and double it.
- If your pulse was more than 130, the exercise was too strenuous.
- A count of 100 indicates a good level of fitness.

The more endurance exercise you do, in conjunction with a low-fat/low-cholesterol diet, the faster you will clean the lining of your arteries. It should be remembered, too, that the incidence of cancer among athletes is only one-seventh the general population. Achieving a clean bloodstream and clean arteries will lead to optimum health, and it can be seen that moderate aerobic exercise is ideal because we are concerned with fat metabolism, particularly if you do not maintain a proper diet. The untrained muscles release lactic acid, which indicates incomplete combustion due to insufficient oxygen and are consequently prone to more discomfort and pain. It is interesting to note that athletes on a high-complex-carbohydrate diet have three times the endurance as athletes on a high-protein and high-fat diet.

The benefits of a fitness program are as follows:

- It increases the capacity of the trained muscles to store glycogen. The main aspect which affects a person's muscular endurance for physical exercise is the amount of glycogen (carbohydrates stored in the muscle tissue).
- It increases the efficiency of fuel combustion.
- It increases the capacity of the muscle to utilise fat, thus sparing glycogen and increasing maximum potential.
- It increases oxygen available for fuel combustion by a way of improved blood supply.

Natural Life and Health

People depend on the sun, and without it, their concentration and work capacity are reduced, and they feel tired. A recent news report from England described a markedly higher performance by schoolchildren whose classrooms were illuminated with ultraviolet-emitting fluorescent lights, instead of incandescent lights. The medical profession is realising that the value of sunshine goes far beyond cheering people up and enabling them to produce vitamin D.

The Immune System

The immune system is the name given to the complex organisation of glands, white blood cells, antibodies and other protein substances, hormones, enzymes, and bacteria which protect the body against potentially harmful germs, viruses, and foreign substances. Such intruders, inert or alive, are called antigens. Even brief bursts of physical activity have the effect of increasing the white blood cell count. The main job of the white cells is to destroy the red cells as they become defective.

In summary, there are two kinds of immune response by the body: the general response against all antigens, and the specific response against each individual antigen, with the specific system providing ongoing immunity against the recurrence of numerous antigens encountered by people throughout life. Now the bottom line is, without the protection of the immune system, death from any number of infections would be swift and certain. At the beginning of life, when a baby's immune system is still being developed, the immune protection is provided by substances in the mother's milk, which is one of the many reasons a baby should be breastfed.

Key point: In the first year of a baby's life, while the immune system and digestive system are still developing, eating certain foods such as cereals, eggs, and pasteurised milk may cause permanent allergies. Why? It is because the undigested food particles which enter the bloodstream confuse the developing immune system, which accepts them as normal in the body.

The dietary substances which mostly inhibit the immune system are fat, cholesterol, and excess protein, all of which are (unfortunately) consumed excessively in our Western world. Vitamin C is important for the proper function of the immune system, and there is generally an inadequate intake of it in our developing nations. Most of us know now that antibiotics have no effect on viruses, which is why herpes and the common cold cannot be cured.

Immunisation

The idea behind immunisation is to artificially provide specific immunity against different disease microbes, by injecting a vaccine made from the microbe, rendering it harmless but still capable of exciting sufficient specific response to produce enough antibodies to create immunity. Here are some amazing facts: In 1796, Edward Jenner of England demonstrated the use of cowpox vaccine against smallpox, and consequently vaccination against smallpox was started. However, despite this, a smallpox epidemic swept England in 1839 and killed 22,089 people. The government in 1853 made smallpox vaccinations compulsory, but the incident of the disease kept increasing, and in 1872, another epidemic killed 44,843 people (most of whom were vaccinated). The compulsory vaccination law was abolished in 1948. Unfortunately, similar disasters happened in Germany and Japan, but the worst was in the Philippines in 1918, when the US government forced over 3,000,000 natives to be vaccinated; of these, 47,369 came down with smallpox and 16,477 died. In 1919, the program was doubled, and over 7,000,000 were vaccinated, of whom 65,180 came down with the disease and 44,408 died. It was shown that the epidemic was a direct result of the vaccination program.

Cancer: A Disease of Civilisation

Cancer is a state of cellular growth which occurs when some normal cells of a plant or animal become abnormal and continue to grow abnormally. The amazing thing is cancer (in the many forms that we know it) is really a disease of modern civilisation, and it is practically unknown among primitive people being nourished on a simple diet.

In 1898, it was reported that the death rate from cancer in England had increased from seventeen per one hundred thousand per year to eighty-eight. In the same period of time, meat consumption had doubled. The solution was to eat more vegetables and get more fresh air and exercise. It is no wonder that the most common form of cancer in Western countries is cancer of the bowel, which includes cancer of the colon and rectum. It is not surprising then that the incidence of cancer is much lower among vegetarians, particularly those who consume no dairy products.

What really happens in cancer patients?

The immune system is defective in varying degrees, and the migrating cancer cells not only survive in the lymph nodes, they proceed to colonise elsewhere in the body as a secondary tumour. This process is called metastasis. Few people actually die from the primary tumour, but once the cancer has metastasised, the condition is usually regarded as terminal.

The Western diet and other civilised indiscretions result in a toxic, fat-clogged bloodstream and eventual liver impairment responsible for the deterioration of the cellular environment, which is known as cancer milieu. Countless people live for years with the cancer milieu without the occurrence of cancer growths, but the advent of severe stress, with its depressing effect on the body's defences, is all that is needed for cancer to advance and grow.

Research has shown that cancer is caused by oxygen deprivation of the cells. As the cancer growth increases, so too do the levels of lactic acid and other toxic waste, which further the toxic milieu, so a vicious circle ensues. The body actually needs more nutritional substances, which it never received and so became overloaded with toxins and started to waste away. This is known as cachexia, which leads to death (usually by pneumonia or heart failure).

What Is Metastasis?

This is where secondary tumours are formed by the cells of the primary growth, which detach and colonise elsewhere in the body. The amazing solution is, metastasis does not occur when the bloodstream is kept free flowing, either by proper diet or the use of blood-thinning drugs. Secondary tumours become quite rapid compared to the primary tumour; doctors call this a terminal condition.

The Role of Diet

All vitamins and minerals are essential, especially vitamins A and E and antioxidants.

In a study of 7,715 cancer patients examined over a fifteen-year period, it was found that 99 percent of them suffered from constipation, and the degree of malignancy paralleled the degree of constipation. It has been observed over a twenty-five-year period in rural Africa that constipation was virtually non-existent, and so too was cancer. Their diet was low in fat and animal protein, was devoid of refined carbohydrates, and contained about three times the amount of vegetable fibre of the English diet. The Western diet is further conducive to cancer in that it not only lacks the necessary fibre, it also lacks the anticarcinogenic substances contained in the missing raw fruit and vegetables.

Protein

Correlations between dietary fat and cancer have been evident for many years, and similar correlations exist with high-protein intake. Cooked protein is difficult to digest, and when incompletely digested protein enters the colon, it putrefies, and ammonia is formed. Ammonia behaves like chemicals that cause cancer or promote its growth. It kills cells, increases virus infection, affects the rate at which cells divide, and increases the mass of the lining of the intestines. What they found in their research is that within the colon, the incidence of cancer paralleled the concentration of ammonia.

Meat

Consumption of meat is strongly suspected to be conducive to cancer. Dr John Berg and associates of the US National Cancer Institute, and Tohoku University School of Medicine in Japan, studied 179 colon cancer patients and found that the consumption of beef was the only factor common to all the cancer patients. In 1977, the International Research on Cancer reported a comparison between Copenhagen and rural Finland. In Copenhagen, the consumption of meat was very high compared to Finland. So not surprisingly in Copenhagen, the incidence of colon cancer was four times higher than in Finland.

Meat not only contributes large amounts of fat, cholesterol and protein, and substances known to be carcinogenic, it contains no fibre and consequently causes constipation.

Salt

Salt is a powerful irritant and a strong inhibitor of enzymes, as well as interfering with circulation by causing fluid retention in the tissues. Even in small quantities, salt has been observed to increase the rate of cancer growth. Research has shown a diet based on whole wheat bread, raw fruit, and vegetables, low in sodium and high in potassium, and no meat, has proven most effective in restoration of cancer patients and patients with all manner of other metabolic diseases.

Vegetables and Herbs

Research has shown that people who ate fewer than two servings of fresh fruit or vegetables a day were three times more likely to develop cancer as people who ate four servings a day.

The Truth about Fluoride

Fluoride is an insidious cumulative poison that strongly suppresses the immune system. There have been a number of occasions where the concentration of fluoride in water has inadvertently reached high levels, resulting in serious sickness through poisoning; some people have actually died. Due to a number of deaths of patients treated on kidney machines using fluoridated water in the United States and Canada, the US surgeon general cautioned all American hospitals to avoid use of fluoridated water in kidney machines.

The Role of Smoking

It is well known that smoking contributes to cancer; here are some amazing facts that are not well known:

- Inhaled carbon monoxide inhibits the oxygen-carrying capacity of the red blood cells.
- Stress is produced in the body.
- The effect these two points increases blood viscosity and reduces blood circulation.
- Carcinogenic chemicals are introduced into the body.
- Smoking destroys vitamin C, essential to collagen, oxygen metabolism, and body detoxification.
- Irritation in the respiratory tract is capable of triggering lung cancer.

The Benefits of Exercise

Aerobic exercises have shown to improve the metabolism of fat, lower blood viscosity, and vastly improve oxygen moving through the body. It has been shown that every single body function becomes more efficient, including the function of the immune system, a most critical factor in cancer.

The Consequences of Stress

Studies have shown that intense and prolonged stress is strongly associated with the onset of cancer. Here are some interesting facts:

- Oxygen available to the tissue cells is decreased because of elevated blood fats and increased blood viscosity, which follows stress.
- It likewise decreases oxygen to the protective white cells of the body's immune system, consequently debilitating them.
- The immune system, consequently stimulated by stress, becomes exhausted and impotent.
- X-rays are known to be a cause of cancer; unfortunately, the people who have many X-rays showed a higher incidence of cancer. In a study of fourteen hundred male adults who had X-rays of the hip, those with twenty or more X-rays had twice the rate of leukaemia than the others.

The Function of the Immune System

If the thymus is debilitated, which is invariable in people who are degenerated, stressed, or sick, the immune system becomes ineffective. The majority of these people are never really in robust health, and the fact that the common cold is indeed very common testifies to the marginal condition of the average person's thymus. The general degeneration of vital organs, accompanied by a lower immune system, which usually accompanies old age, accounts for the increase in cancer in older age groups. Tonsils and the appendix are important components of the immune system, and although the body can get by without them, a certain degree of protection is lost.

Cancer of the Bowel (Colon and Rectum)

Unfortunately, this form of cancer is the most common form in the West and causes the most cancer deaths. Countries with the highest consumption of beef (Australia, the United States, Canada, New Zealand, England, Scotland, and Argentina) all suffer from a high incidence of bowel cancer. Scotland has the highest bowel cancer rate in the world, with the worst incidence around Aberdeen, the cattle-raising centre. The Scottish consume 19 percent more beef per capita than the English, and their bowel cancer rate is precisely 19 percent greater than the English.

Breast Cancer

Breast cancer is much higher in countries where people eat high-fat diets. Breast cancer is the number one cause of death in women aged thirty-five to fifty in the United States. It is interesting to note that Holland and Denmark have seven times the rate of Japan, with its low-fat diet.

Cancer of the Stomach

Japan and Iceland have the highest stomach cancer rates in the world. The Japanese average one ounce of salt per day and have a very high rate of hypertension. Icelanders eat a lot of smoked fish and smoked meat. In a study of sixteen hundred deaths caused by stomach cancer, the highest incidence correlated with the consumption of smoked meat. It is interesting to note that nitrates are used as preservatives of processed meats, ham, bacon, and frankfurters. The problem is, nitrates can be changed in the stomach to nitrosamines, some of which are carcinogenic.

Cancer of the Liver

Primary cancer of the liver may occur when sclerosis exists and the liver tissue is attempting to restore itself. It is now well known that heavy drinkers and smokers are likely candidates. As I have said before, people in undeveloped countries who eat more natural foods escape most of these problems.

Why Is Lung Cancer So Dangerous?

Until recently, lung cancer has caused more deaths among men than any other form of cancer (it has now been overtaken by cancer of the bowel). Smoking not only brings carcinogenic tars and other irritants into the lungs, it also elevates blood fats by its effect on the nervous system and simultaneously reduces oxygen available to the tissues by carbon monoxide poisoning of the red blood cells. In Chicago, in a survey of 878 smokers with high cholesterol levels, the lung cancer rate was thirty-seven per thousand; for those with medium cholesterol levels, the lung cancer rate was only five per thousand; but for those smokers with a low cholesterol level, there was no cancer at all.

Key point: Research has found that non-smokers, in social contact with smokers, will inhale, whether they like it or not, 50 percent as much carbon monoxide as if they were smoking. The amazing fact is carbon monoxide is more harmful than the tar in nicotine.

Cancer of the Mouth, Larynx, and Oesophagus

This cancer, like all others, stems from a faulty diet. Heavy drinkers are susceptible, and their risk is magnified if they smoke as well. In some countries where this cancer is common, the irritation is caused by heavily spiced or very hot food. Cancer of the oesophagus is common in certain areas of Iran, where the diet consists almost entirely of coarse bread. The problem is compounded by dietary deficiencies, where there is little or no fruit or vegetables available.

Leukaemia

Leukaemia is the uncontrolled proliferation of white blood cells in the body and bloodstream. It occurs mainly in young people. A common thread that was shown in tests was that leukaemia patients all displayed low levels of vitamin C.

Prostate Cancer

Cancer of the prostate is usually preceded by a benign condition in which the prostate has become enlarged. The enlargement is caused mainly by accumulation of cholesterol crystals.

Cancer of the Uterus

This form of cancer is associated with obesity; women who are twenty kilograms or more overweight are ten times more likely to get cancer of the uterus. The highest risk category, however, is overweight women with diabetes.

Skin Cancer

It is generally accepted that most skin cancers are caused by overexposure to the sun. Skin cancer is greater in countries with sunny climates and more common among fair-skinned people. Studies have shown that skin cancer does not readily occur among people on very low-fat/low-cholesterol diets.

Kidney Cancer

Australia has the highest incidence of kidney disease and kidney cancer in the world. This is caused by not only the excessive intake of protein, fat, and cholesterol, but also the enormous consumption of painkillers.

How Stress Affects Your Body

We are now going to look at stress and how it affects your life, in depth. Research has shown that humans activate the stress response for reasons of a psychological nature, and we are simply not designed for that. The bottom line is that we all act differently to the same amount of stress.

Stress and Your Heart

In life-threatening situations, your body sends blood to where it is needed, to the thigh muscles and the lungs, and at the same time, it diverts blood away from the parts of the body that do not need it, such as your stomach and reproductive organs. When blood pressure is increasing, the blood vessels respond by building up more muscle. This makes the blood vessels more rigid, which consequently requires more force to get the blood through, so the body increases the blood pressure, and that starts a vicious cycle called hypertension. When you get enough slamming of the blood against the walls of the blood vessels, small amounts of damage begin to appear in tearing and scarring, which causes inflammation and plaque to form. Now, along comes the fat and the glucose and the cholesterol, and that is more likely to stick onto this inflamed plaque. Very interesting research has shown that if you combine hypertension with a high-fat diet, you will get far more vascular damage than if they were separate.

Another potential problem is diabetes. If you have got type 1 diabetes and are chronically stressed, this starts a vicious cycle: Every time you get stressed, you are releasing a flow of sugar into your bloodstream, and then it is stored away, and that is the very opposite of what blood sugar control is all about. It causes the blood sugar level to oscillate. The bottom line: chronic stress makes glycaemic control (control of sugar) more precarious for a person with diabetes. Type 2 diabetes is becoming much more prevalent in Western societies. The problem here is not too little insulin; it is an excess of nutrients caused by putting on weight and being more sedentary. A definition of diabetes will help to clarify all of this:

Type 1 diabetes is an autoimmune disorder in which the pancreas is unable to secrete insulin.

Type 2 diabetes is a disorder, typically brought on by obesity, in which cells throughout the body have become resistant to insulin. Insulin is a hormone released from the pancreas that promotes the storage of glucose throughout the body. It is normally secreted when blood glucose levels rise; however, secretion is inhibited in the early stages of stress.

Stress and Overeating

If you spend all day having moments of stress, you will spend a lot of time recovering from it. The consequences are, your appetite increases, and generally you crave carbohydrates (that is, bread, sugars, treats, and chocolate). Abdominal fat is more dangerous for a whole bunch of reasons. It releases inflammatory signals which can be a greater risk in your torso than other parts of your body; it sits close to your liver, which could lead to a fatty liver; and its pressure pulls your spine forward. Abdominal fat puts more stress on your body.

Stress and Child Development

Research has shown in stress situations, your blood pressure goes up to deliver energy to the thigh muscles, but the blood flow decreases to the unessential areas of the stomach. If a child is suffering from stress, the chronically decreasing blood flow to the stomach would keep nutrients from being properly absorbed. In children, growth hormone plays a huge role in depositing new calcium in the bones.

If chronic stress is experienced, growth hormone levels drop, and less calcium is deposited into the bones. Unfortunately, this scenario will cause brittle, prematurely aging bones and osteoporosis later in life.

Stress and Memory

Studies have shown that sustained stress changes the structure of neurons in the hippocampus, which causes them to atrophy. The amazing fact is, in the short term, stress is a great thing for your learning and memory, but in the long term, it is very debilitating.

Stress and the Lack of Sleep

All doctors agree that sleep restores energy, particularly to your brain. The brain constitutes about 3 percent of your body weight, but it uses 25 percent of your body's energy, and brain cells (neurons) have virtually no capacity to store energy, so sleep is especially useful in restoring energy to the brain.

Stress and Aging

It has been shown that lots of stress makes you get older faster, and being older and more fragile makes you less able to deal with stress. Aging is a time of life when you do not deal very well with stress, and the price you pay is decreased DNA repair, decreased ability to regulate temperature, and decreased cognitive ability. The bottom line is, lots of stress over your lifetime will accelerate the aging process. Lots of stress also reduces memory recall.

Psychological Levels of Stress

Contrary to popular belief, it is not upper management who are getting stress-related diseases, it is actually middle management. A key feature of middle management is that they have high demand and low control: high demand in that they are in a position of great responsibility, but low control because they are not the one making policy. Also, people who have low demand and low control are stressed because these people have a lack of control plus boredom; for the people in upper management, as long as they are doing a job that they like, the high degree of control and high degree of demand makes it a great combination.

Stress and Depression

Depression is the loss of capacity to feel pleasure. The World Health Organisation stated that depression is the fourth leading cause of disability in the world. By 2020, it is expected to be in second place. There is a tendency for people who are highly depressed to injure themselves, to attempt suicide, or to actually succeed in committing suicide. Depression also changes the appetite and, in many cases, metabolism as well. Men when depressed are more likely than women to self-medicate with alcohol and other drugs; they are more likely to be labelled an alcoholic than a depressed person. On average, women have higher rates of depression than do men, and it seems to peak during the two weeks after giving birth, around menopause, and around the time of the menstrual cycle. The reason is that in these circumstances, there are very dramatic changes in levels of certain hormones. It has been shown that people who have had a string of major stressful events are more likely to fall into a state of depression.

Stress, Health, and Low Social Status

Studies have shown that these three issues are inextricably linked; the underlying problem is that people in the low social economic category work two or three jobs or spend all of their time trying to fix items that were broken. It was shown, for example, in the greater Washington DC area, life expectancy of inner city residents was sixteen years less than those in the wealthier suburbs. The bottom line is that poor people have poor health and drink more alcohol than wealthy people; they smoke more, eat to excess, and get less exercise. The amazing thing is, research has shown that feeling poor has at least as much impact as being poor.

Stress Management Solutions

All researchers agree that having a healthy lifestyle is the answer. Smoking, being overweight, not getting enough exercise, and drinking too much all shorten life expectancy. Having a long-lasting good marriage, however, is very therapeutic. Researchers also discovered that nursing home residents felt better when given some responsibility, like watering plants. They clearly enjoyed the responsibility of having to water the plants every day. One of the most effective things to do, of course, is exercise. They found that exercise also stimulates the neurons and makes them grow new connections.

There are certain qualifications, however. You cannot just save your stress management for the weekend; it must be done daily. In regard to aerobic exercise, most studies suggest you need to do twenty to thirty minutes to get the cardiovascular advantages. Most importantly, you have got to enjoy doing it. They also found that meditation lowers the heart rate and blood pressure as well as cholesterol levels, particularly the LDL cholesterol.

Another factor was having social support: being around people you love and trust, such as church, family, and friends. It was also found that for men, getting married actually improved their immune system; for women, it was not so simple: It had to be a good marriage. Studies showed also that religious beliefs tended to increase protection against cardiovascular disease and depression, and they increased life expectancy.

The Science of Natural Healing

We are now going to look at the wonderful healing properties of food, but before we do, we should review the greatest culprit of the Western diet: refining food. Refining food removes important vitamins and minerals. For example, the refining process removes 77 percent of thiamine, which can only be obtained through food; 76 percent of iron, which is needed to make red blood cells; and 85 percent of magnesium, which is needed not only to keep our bowels moving, but also to keep our heart healthy. When food is refined, it removes copper, zinc, and calcium: everything that we need to have strong and healthy bones.

One of the greatest things that whole foods give us is fibre. Fibre is found in beans, peas, nuts, apples, and vegetables. Fibre is important in lowering cholesterol and blood sugar. It works by binding the fatty acids in the intestine and pulls them out of the body. Fibre also blocks the quick absorption of sugar.

Vegetables

Let's look at some advantages of vegetables:

- Broccoli contains sulforaphane, which is an anticancer food that eliminates toxins from our body.

- Spinach is very high in antioxidants, and research shows that it is good for the eyes.
- Lycopene occurs in tomatoes and aids against prostate cancer. It can even lower blood pressure and block platelets from sticking together (the first step towards having a heart attack is when the platelets stick together).
- Blueberries contain anthocyanosides, which protect the eyes and give you a potent antioxidant, which is good for the heart and blocks bacteria from sticking to the lining of your bladder.

Nuts

Nuts are a source of fibre and protein and also contain magnesium, zinc, calcium, and vitamin E, which is an antioxidant. Walnuts have over sixteen polyphenols, which are photo nutrients with strong antioxidant capabilities. They help protect our heart and lungs.

Causes of Inflammation

Inflammation is the body's normal response to an injury, infection, stress, foreign substance, and anything that may be irritating us. Research has shown cancer, Alzheimer's disease, and heart disease are all linked to inflammation. It may be surprising that most cardiologists today are less worried about cholesterol, as it relates to a blockage in the arteries, than about inflammation. Inflammation is more important. Polluted air, chemical irritants, second-hand smoke, and pesticides are all seen by the body as foreign invaders. Ulcers are chronic infections and are caused by bacterium called helicobacter pylori. This bacterium sits in the stomach and produces inflammation; it can cause ulcers and even stomach cancer.

Another common cause of inflammation is having too much weight around the midline. Those fat cells are actually an inflammatory organ, and they produce cytokines, which raise blood pressure, cause inflammation, and can make you diabetic.

People with sleep apnoea snore and often stop breathing while sleeping. This can also lead to chronic inflammation and weight gain.

Food and Inflammation

There are eight major foods that contribute to inflammation:

1. The number one cause of inflammation is sugar, which exists in the form of corn syrup, dextrose, fructose, golden syrup, maltose, and sucrose.
2. Stay clear of oils that are high in omega 6 such as grapeseed oil, cottonseed oil, corn oil, safflower oil, and sunflower oil. These are industrial vegetable oils that are usually found in fast foods and processed oils. Remember: Olive oil becomes toxic when it is heated.
3. Trans fats are a modified form of fat that increases and oxidises the bad cholesterol (that is, LDL).
4. Cow's milk also leads to inflammation. People who are lactose intolerant typically develop diarrhoea, gas, and bloating.
5. Cured meats and red meats contain a substance called Neu5Gc, which is a compound that the body sees as a foreign invader, so it produces antibodies and triggers an inflammatory response.
6. Excessive alcohol consumption is rampant in our culture and is linked to irritation and inflammation of the oesophagus. High consumption of alcohol affects the liver, from cirrhosis to alcohol-induced hepatitis.
7. Another cause of inflammation is consumption of refined grains, such as white bread and white rice.
8. Other artificial food additives, such as monosodium glutamate (MSG) and aspartame, cause inflammation.

Preventing Inflammation

To prevent inflammation, eat whole foods: fish high in omega 3, kelp (seaweed), and whole fruits and vegetables. Use olive oil, avocado oil, and macadamia nut oil, instead of oil made from corn. Drink filtered water, but do not drink water from plastic bottles; it is not good for your health. Green tea can protect against cancer; it is anti-inflammatory and can reduce cardiovascular disease. Herbs and spices, when used correctly, are powerful anti-inflammatory components. Turmeric also has anticancer properties. Ginger is a spice that has powerful anti-inflammatory benefits and also helps with nausea.

Food Allergies

An allergic reaction to a food can happen quickly; for example, if someone who is allergic eats shellfish or a peanut, they will all of a sudden be unable to breathe. There are also low-grade allergies; for example, you keep on taking a certain food, and your body keeps seeing it as a foreign invader, and consequently it works consistently to clear the toxin from your system. Even though the reaction may not seem so severe, the long-term consequences are enormous.

Fatigue, trouble sleeping, mental fogginess, mood changes, irritability, anger, skin irritation, and rashes are common signs of food sensitivity.

Arthritis, muscle stiffness, and joint pains can be caused by the protein in cow's milk. It is not just about having gas and bloating. Research has shown that food sensitivity is connected to six common groups: dairy, gluten, corn, soy, peanuts, and egg.

Key point: You can buy gluten-free bread, such as bread made from organic brown rice.

Vitamins and Supplements

Always remember that supplements are just that: supplements. They are not a replacement for proper nutrition and a healthy lifestyle.

The Benefits of Natural Products

Probiotics are found in yogurt, kefir, and many other food items. A probiotic is a living organism that, when ingested in the right amounts, can have a healthy benefit. One of the most serious inflammatory diseases is ulcerated colitis, which can make someone's life miserable by causing dehydration, nausea, gas, bloating, and diarrhoea. Probiotics help to fight against flare-ups of ulcerated colitis. People who have gastroenteritis often experience diarrhoea, which causes dehydration because of a loss of fluids. Potassium and magnesium are also lost, which is why they feel so terrible. Probiotics help to significantly reduce the risk and duration of diarrhoea.

Selenium, which is another natural supplement, has been helpful in reducing prostate cancer. Vitamin D (which is not really a vitamin but a hormone) is needed for your bones and heart. It protects your muscles and helps with depression and symptoms of fibromyalgia, such as muscle aching. Low levels of vitamin D can lead to calcification on the valves of the heart.

Key point: Taking four grams of omega 3 fish oil daily will lower your triglycerides, which is the form of fat that comes from sugar and white foods, by 45 percent.

Herbs

We are now going to look at the wonderful effects that herbs can have on the body through natural healing. Here are a few examples:

- Aloe vera is used to treat burns and wounds externally, but it can also treat inflammation internally (for example, inflammation in the mouth from chemotherapy).
- Ginger is used to treat nausea and vomiting from pregnancy, chemotherapy, and travel sickness. (The National Cancer Institute showed a 40 percent reduction in chemotherapy-induced nausea when people were given one gram of ginger three days prior to their chemotherapy treatment.)
- Amazingly, licorice is one of the best herbal remedies for heartburn, which twenty-five million Americans suffer from. The key to actually preventing heartburn is to stop eating heartburn-causing foods such as cooked tomato sauce, excess caffeine, chocolate, carbonated beverages, fried foods, alcohol, and foods that are very high in fat, including full-fat dairy products.
- Peppermint is an herbal remedy for irritable bowel syndrome (IBS). This very common disorder affects the large intestine. The signs of irritable bowel syndrome are cramping, pain, bloating, gas, diarrhoea, and constipation.
- Research has shown that saw palmetto significantly improves symptoms in people who have mild to moderate enlargement of their prostate gland; the benefits are, they get up less at night to urinate, and the urinary stream is stronger.

Lowering Cholesterol Naturally

So what is cholesterol? It is a waxy substance found in the fats in your blood. The body needs cholesterol to make healthy cells, but having high LDL cholesterol can increase the risk of heart disease. Not all cholesterol is bad; high-density lipoprotein (HDL) is the good cholesterol. This cholesterol pulls plaque out of the arteries.

Triglycerides are a type of fat that circulates in our bloodstream. They store unused calories, so if we go for a long time without food, the triglycerides are able to release the energy from this stored fat when we need it. Triglycerides build up because of a lack of exercise and from overeating. Sugar, including alcohol, fruit juice, and soda, also contributes to high triglyceride levels, which is really unused calories.

There are three simple steps to lower your triglycerides: nutrition, exercise, and supplements. Cut out sugar and simple carbohydrates, as these raise the triglycerides. The best foods to eat that will lower your triglycerides are whole grains, lentils, beans, and fruits that are low in sugar, such as apples, peaches, pears, plums, berries, oranges, and grapefruits. Green leafy vegetables and omega 3s can also lower your triglycerides. It has been shown that omega 3 fish oil decreases triglycerides by 45 percent, if you take four grams (or four thousand milligrams) per day.

How to Lower the Bad Cholesterol

Reduce intake of the following foods, and you will reduce LDL cholesterol: beef, pork, lamb, cheese, full-fat yogurt, butter, and cream. Lower your LDL cholesterol by substituting meat with vegetable protein, which has zero cholesterol.

Key point: Keep away from shrimp, as it is extremely high in cholesterol; instead, eat salmon or sardines.

How to Treat High Blood Pressure Naturally

High blood pressure is often referred to as the silent killer because most people are unaware of its presence. Blood pressure is simply the force of blood exerted against the walls of your arteries. The best way to lower your blood pressure naturally is to decrease your weight. This is achieved by proper nutrition and exercise. Exercise is basically good medicine because it increases lean muscle mass and bone density and therefore decreases weight, which consequently reduces blood pressure. Alcohol actually raises blood pressure and increases appetite. It is a sugar and should be restricted. One cup of coffee per day is the maximum you should drink if you want to lower your blood pressure. Organic green tea is a much better choice, as it is an antioxidant.

Sodium (or salt) is one of the main issues of the Western diet. Most people take in ten times the amount their body actually needs: 5,000 mg of sodium per day, instead of just 500 mg. Salt is in packaged and canned foods, and it is also hidden in just about every item on a restaurant menu. Blood pressure can also be lowered by eating garlic and tomatoes; lycopene, which is the active ingredient in tomatoes, has been proven to lower blood pressure. Blood pressure can be further reduced by adding more omega 3s, such as fish, and eliminating saturated fats.

How to Treat Diabetes Naturally

What is insulin? It is a hormone that controls blood sugar and is produced by the pancreas. Insulin resistance occurs when sugar is no longer properly transported into cells. The problem is, the pancreas then has to keep working harder and harder to produce more insulin; eventually, it becomes exhausted and cannot produce the required amount. That is when people need insulin injections.

Most people do not realise that lack of sleep can lead to insulin resistance. Why? Because lack of sleep puts stress on the body, and stress raises blood sugar and makes insulin resistance worse. Research has shown that people who get five hours of sleep or less have a higher risk of developing diabetes. Good nutrition is the key to preventing (and even reversing) diabetes. Doctors often refer to the glycaemic index; the higher the index, the faster the body converts food to sugar.

Green leafy vegetables have a very low glycaemic index; vegetables such as cauliflower, broccoli, and cabbage are all good choices. Other good choices would be omega 3 fish such as salmon, mackerel, sardines, and herring. Carrots also have a low glycaemic index and are very high in fibre, which actually slows down the absorption of sugar and lowers blood pressure.

If you are trying to lower your blood sugar level, you need to find healthier alternatives for cakes, chocolate, and ice cream. You should also not drink soft drinks, fruit juice, and alcohol.

Garlic and onions help to bring down blood sugar levels; focus on eating green leafy vegetables with a light amount of olive oil or turmeric dressing.

Preventing and Reversing Diabetes (Physical Activity)

On average, people in the Western world spend six hours per day in front of a TV or computer, so you must make time for exercise. We know now that exercise builds muscle, decreases insulin resistance, decreases blood pressure, improves cholesterol, and makes us feel better. Also, one of the best benefits of exercise is that it helps you sleep better.

Connection among Mind, Body, and Stress

Research has shown that 90 percent of all visits to health care providers is because of stress-related disorders.

Stress is experienced when people don't feel that they can do everything that it is expected of them. When under stress, the body goes through physiological changes that are actually measured and quantified; for example, there is an increase in heart rate, blood sugar, breathing rate, and blood pressure. If we never turn away from stress, our blood pressure increases, and consequently, we end up with stomach ulcers and are more prone to infections and even cancer itself.

The Mental and Emotional Effects of Stress

Stress causes not only physical changes, but also emotional and mental changes. Research has shown that people under stress have cognitive inhibition, which results in them not making the best choices; they subsequently lose their focus and sense of clarity.

Stress causes people's bodies to release adrenaline and cortisol into their bloodstream. Adrenaline goes away when the anxiety eases, but cortisol does not, and this causes people to want to eat more carbohydrates to replace the energy they have just lost, and so they gain weight.

Stress affects our ability to relax and sleep, and when we feel that we cannot cope, stress even affects our self-esteem. Stress also leads to anger, which increases the risk of heart attack by up to 230 percent, so we can see that anger is one of the most lethal emotions that can cause a heart attack. We know now that under stress, the immune system is affected and blood sugar increases; it also exacerbates diabetes.

Making Stress Your Strength

Stress per se is not really the problem; it is your mental and emotional reactions to the problem. Research has shown that people with a positive mental attitude, that is the optimists, have increased longevity. The key is not just thinking about a positive emotion, but actually feeling a positive emotion, which has positive effects on your body.

People who are generally negative should try keeping a gratefulness journal; at the end of the day, they should write down things that they were grateful for, so they start to feel more contented and consequently obtain a physiological benefit from these positive emotions. The bottom line is, adding the power of positive emotions can improve your cognition, increase your mental powers, and help in making decisions. One of the best keys to do this is to think about a special place that you enjoy or someone you love and appreciate.

Research has also shown that people who learn to meditate on the Bible, have a significant reduction in anxiety. They feel less stressed, less anxious, and less worried.

Natural Approaches to Good Health

The human brain is fuelled by molecules that come from our diet, and just as in the case with the rest of our body, some of the foods we eat promote brain health, while others may actually do harm. Processed food actually removes essential vitamins and minerals, so make sure that you eat whole foods; for example, folic acid, which is essential to a healthy brain, is found in whole grains.

There is mounting evidence that links omega 3 deficiency to a number of disorders, including depression and bipolar disorder. The Avon Longitudinal Study of Parents and Children showed that a diet high in vegetables, fruit, fish, and grains was associated with a lower rate of depression and anxiety. A comprehensive study of over ten thousand adults showed that the more fruits, nuts, legumes, and monounsaturated fats that were consumed, the more the amount of depression was reduced. It also showed that there was a link between depression and bipolar disorder in diets with a high glycaemic index (diets that are high in simple sugars and simple carbohydrates). According to a 1996 study in *The Lancet*, gluten sensitivity was a contributing factor in schizophrenia, bipolar disorder, and anxiety.

Magnesium deficiency has been shown to cause depression; this came from a study of over five thousand people. So how do we get more magnesium naturally? It comes from eating green leafy vegetables.

People with vitamin D deficiency were found to be more depressed than the general population. One of the ways to treat depression naturally is to have more folate, which is in the B group vitamins. It was also shown that St John's wort, used as an herbal remedy, is effective for mild to moderate depression. The bottom line is that exercising in the sunlight is good for treating depression.

The Power of Good Relationships

Amazingly, scientific studies have shown that people who had strained relationships with their parents increased their health risk significantly. This includes heart disease, cancer, ulcers, and hypertension. To their surprise, people with close and warm relationships cut their health risk from 100 to 40 percent.

A study of unhappy marriages involving nine thousand British civil servants over a period of twelve years showed a 34 percent increase in heart problems, regardless of their social status or gender. It pays to be an optimist because research showed that they had a 55 percent chance of a longer life and 23 percent lower risk of heart problems.

The Bible says it is better to give than to receive, and researchers found that those who gave love and support had fewer health problems.

How Your Spiritual Life Affects Your Health

Research has shown that highly religious people had a 29 percent higher survival rate compared to nonreligious people. They also found that those who attended at least one religious service a week lived a longer life. These people were seen to have more health advantages because in general, they had more people supporting them and tended to have increased hope, more contentment, and more peace. The Bible says, "Godliness with contentment is great gain" (1 Timothy 6:6).

It is not surprising that depression and hopelessness are the same bedfellows; depression causes a 40 percent increase in heart disease.

The Bible says that forgiveness is for your sake, as it releases you from future bitterness and leads to better health. It reduces blood pressure, causes less tension in the muscles, and produces a slower heart rate. This leads to fewer illnesses and fewer chronic conditions. People who practise forgiveness are more optimistic, less angry, and less stressed.

Jesus said so cogently, "For as he thinks in his heart so is he." Prov.23:7a NKJV. Some findings of this positive thinking study were that people had a lower rate of depression and stress, greater resistance to the common cold, and fewer heart attacks, and they coped a lot better through times of hardship.

Pollution and Health

These two are inextricably linked; the underlying problem is, one billion people lack access to fresh clean water. Most health experts agree that you should drink eight glasses of clean water per day, or 2 litres. Pollution, is estimated to cause 1.3 million deaths worldwide per year. Air pollution is one of the largest causes of cardiovascular disease.

What You Can Do to Improve Your Health

Always buy organic fruits and vegetables (or grow your own). Why? Because there are over 450 pesticides and herbicides used on nonorganic products. The problem is that farmers overuse their soil and greatly deplete it of its nutrients. Organic farmers, however, practice crop rotation, which gives the soil much more time to recover and replenish its nutrients. Another good way to improve your health is, don't store hot foods in plastic containers because the toxins from the plastic will leach into your food. The answer is to use glass or porcelain; don't use plastic in a microwave. Another inexpensive way to improve your health is simply going for a walk; the benefits are many: You lose weight, it counters depression, and it improves your quality of sleep.

The Consequences of Eating Sugar

Now, we are going to have an in-depth look at the history of sugar and its consequences in the Western diet. It has been referred to by some as "sweet poison." Sugar consumption in England rose eightfold between 1815 and 1955. Consumption in the British Isles has gone from seven kilograms of sugar per annum in 1817 to fifty kilograms per annum in 1955. The problem is that when sugar is refined from cane or sugar beet, 99 percent of the original food (mostly the fibre) is removed, leaving only the sugar syrup.

Let's look at three different food groups and what happens to them when they are broken down:

This food ...	Contains ...	Which breaks down to ...
Milk and dairy foods	Lactose	Galactose + glucose
Beer	Maltose	Glucose + glucose
Table sugar, brown sugar, caster sugar	Sucrose	Glucose + fructose

We can see that milk and dairy products contain lactose, and lactose intolerance causes diarrhoea and flatulence.

Here is a chart that shows that the whole world looks like glucose to our digestive system:

Snapshot of what happens to food:

This food …	Contains (mostly) …	Which breaks down to …
Bread	Carbohydrate	Glucose + fibre
Milk	Carbohydrate + fat	Glucose + galactose + fatty acids
Meat (or nuts)	Protein + fat	Glucose + amino acids + fatty acids
Fruit	Carbohydrate	Glucose + fructose + fibre
Vegetables	Carbohydrate	Glucose + fibre

With regard to meat, we know that leftover amino acids are converted to glucose and used for energy in exactly the same way as carbohydrates. The remaining third of our food is fat. Insulin is a powerful hormone that regulates the digestive system, but its main function is to reduce glucose concentrations in our blood. We now know that without the presence of insulin in the blood, the cells have no chemical means of assessing the energy stored as glucose. Insulin, therefore, acts as a chemical enabler, it allows the cells to absorb and then convert the glucose to energy (the exception is the brain because it absorbs the glucose directly from the bloodstream).

Key point: About one in every fifty thousand people is unable to make insulin. These people have insulin-dependent diabetes (also called type 1 diabetes). The technical term is hyperglycaemia ("hyper-" is excessive, "glyc-" is sweet; "aemia" is related to the blood); the brain is the only major organ able to use glucose without insulin.

Stored glucose in the form of glycogen helps to smooth out our energy requirements; amazingly, without it, we would have to eat every four hours or risk running out of the glucose fuel required to keep our brain and internal organs functioning.

It is a known fact that eating sugar causes uric acid levels to rise. Uric acid is the by-product of starving the body of carbohydrates, forcing it to switch to protein and fat metabolism. If the problem is prolonged, excess uric acid production eventually leads to high blood acidity; that does a lot of damage to the eyes and kidneys and fragile organs in people with diabetes.

Research has found that people who feed on large amounts of sugar have "sticky" blood, and that causes massive blood clots, leading to heart attacks. The incidence of heart disease is parallel with the rise in consumption of sugar.

Research has also shown that small amounts of fructose will start the glucose to digest in the liver. This can occur after eating two of pieces of fruit. If we eat a high-fructose diet, the fructose will be converted directly to fatty acids and, in turn, to body fat.

Fructose does not release any of the "had-enough-to-eat" hormones. It skips the fat-creation mechanism in the liver; fructose is directly converted to fatty acids (body fat), without passing through our appetite control gateways. The problem is every gram of fructose we eat is directly converted to fat.

Eating fat still puts fat in our arteries, but we have a built-in control to stop us eating too much fat. No such control exists for fructose; remember: sugar is half fructose. We now know that once refined and concentrated, sugar is more than six times as sweet as an apple, which is the sweetest, most commonly known fruit.

The production of sugar has really rocketed in Australia. For example, at the end of World War II, Australia was producing 950,000 tonnes per annum. In 1954, it was producing 2.3 million tonnes, and by 1980, it was 3 million tonnes. By 2000, Australia was producing more than 6.4 million tonnes. Amazingly, today, Australia exports 85 percent of its sugar crop, making it the second-largest sugar exporter in the world, behind Brazil.

In the 1830s, when the world population had just passed one billion, on average each person consumed eight hundred grams of sugar per year. By 1975, when the world's population was just over four billion, each person consumed twenty kilograms per year, so that means that people were consuming twenty-five times more sugar than their great-grandfathers did, just 140 years earlier.

In 1885, the average adult in the United States consumed thirteen kilograms of added fructose in the form of twenty-five kilograms of sugar, a substance that their parents had never seen, let alone tasted. By 1909, US sugar consumption was forty kilograms per person, per year, and by 1932, Americans were eating almost fifty kilograms of sugar per year.

By the end of World War II, the average American was drinking 38 litres of carbonated soft drink each year; that represented 9 percent of their entire sugar for the year. By 1965, they were drinking twice as much soft drink, and it represented 18 percent of the entire sugar they were consuming each year. By 1985, soft drink consumption had doubled again. In the early 1980s, Coke and Pepsi decided to switch from sugar to high-fructose corn syrup (HFCS). The reason they did this was HFCS was cheap, so they could produce supersized proportions at little cost, and subsequently increased their profits. Now, soft drinks in America represent 35 percent of all the sugar consumed in a year.

Americans are eating 33.0 kilograms of fructose, each year compared to 22.5 kilograms in Australia, 50 percent in each case is converted to body fat each year. We are fighting a losing battle as both countries do not want to give up their soft drinks and advertising keeps reinforcing this addiction.

Body Mass Index

The BMI is calculated by taking our weight in kilograms, divided by the square of our height in centimetres. Adults are considered overweight when their BMI is between 25 and 29.9; obesity starts at 30. In 1910, just over one in five adults in the United States was overweight, and one in twenty-five were obese. About a century later, two out of three adults in the United States were overweight, and one-third were obese.

The sad fact is that four out of five Generation X (born 1966–1975) Americans will actually be obese and not just overweight, by age seventy, in around 2036. A person with a normal BMI will indeed be rare.

The biggest killer in Australia today is cardiovascular heart disease; it is mostly due to blocked arteries, medically known as atherosclerosis (from the Greek "*athera*," meaning "porridge," and "*skleros*," meaning hard. The bottom line is that these blockages are formed from the exact fatty acids created by the overconsumption of fructose.

In Australia, forty-eight thousand people will die from cardiovascular disease this year; that is over thirty times as many as will die in car accidents and over three hundred times as many as will die from AIDS. In comparison, the United States will have 650,000 people die from cardiovascular disease.

The sad fact is that this year, one-quarter of all Australians with heart disease will experience their first heart attack and then they will die. The main culprit is a blood clot that either blocks the artery totally or causes the heart muscle to die; either way, the end result is a heart attack.

Research has shown that prior to 1930, less than 2 percent of people died from a heart attack. In 1949, that figure rose to 8 percent, and in 1959, the figure jumped to 27 percent. Fifty-five years later, after the introduction of sugar used in commercial quantities, 30 percent of deaths attributed to heart attacks were caused by fat blocking the arteries. Further US studies have shown that heart attacks were almost nonexistent as a cause of death in 1900, and they caused no more than three thousand deaths per year by 1930. By 1960, this had jumped to half a million deaths in the United States.

The next major killer is stroke, which kills thousands of people every year. A stroke is simply a disruption of the blood supply to the brain. Brain cells can survive about four minutes without oxygen. Note: Only 33 percent of stroke sufferers die as a result of stroke, whereas 90 percent of heart attack sufferers die.

Bypass operations are on the rise; by 1980, almost four thousand bypass operations were being performed annually. This jumped to eighteen thousand per year by 2000. In America, however, by the year 2007, five hundred thousand bypass operations were performed. The bottom line is, about 50 percent of the Australian population continue to have high cholesterol today. We have not cured the problem. We are just getting better at making sure that fewer people die from it.

A Deadly Hazard

Fructose has created type 2 diabetes because of our insatiable appetite for sweet things. In 2008, thirty-five hundred Australians died because of diabetes; that was twice as many people as were killed on our roads that year.

Type 2 diabetes originally only affected older people, as it only occurred later in life. The real problem is that the number of overweight people in the Western world has increased at an earlier age. Type 2 diabetes is now showing up in teenagers and even in younger children.

Studies have shown over the last thirty years that fructose consumption definitely results in insulin resistance.

The International Diabetes Federation estimated that in 2003, about 194 million people on the planet had diabetes. They predict that this will grow to 333 million by 2025. Insulin resistance affected 314 million people in 2003, and that number is expected to grow to 472 million by 2025. Note: In less than twenty years, almost one billion people worldwide will be affected by this life-threatening disease that was virtually unheard of thirty years ago. Research further found that fifty to sixty years of continuously eating fructose leads to a high likelihood of heart attack or stroke.

In virtually every developed nation, type 2 diabetes is a leading cause of blindness, kidney failure, and limb amputation. As we have already discovered, there is a significant risk factor of death from heart disease. Shockingly, there is a death due to type 2 diabetes every six seconds worldwide and an amputation caused by diabetes every thirty seconds.

Does Exercise Help?

There is no doubt that exercise greatly improves your overall health, but exercise alone will not allow you to lose significant amounts of weight if you continue to eat large amounts of fructose. We know that overweight people do less exercise because they are overweight, and they are overweight because they do less exercise. It is basically a simple matter of mathematics; if you eat more calories than you spend, you will gain weight. Try to remember to move more and eat less.

If You Consume	Or	Do This Exercise
Can of soft drink	150 calories	Ride a bicycle eight kilometre
Chocolate bar	294 calories	Swim laps for an hour
Fast-food burger	515 calories	Run six kilometres

Here are some interesting facts: 14 percent of our energy needs are supplied by proteins; 53 percent of our energy needs are supplied by carbohydrates; 33 percent of our energy needs come from fat found in meats and vegetable oils. One gram of fat yields about twice as much energy as either protein or carbohydrate.

The bottom line is, our extraordinarily efficient production of energy means that increasing our physical exercise is less efficient in reducing weight than the amount of food we consume. The average male only needs twenty-five hundred calories per day, and the average female only two thousand calories. Fructose is the overlooked culprit in fat reduction; for example, of the ninety-six calories found in apple juice, the hypothalamus only sees the thirty-two calories provided by the glucose. The sixty-four calories provided by the fructose goes completely undetected by the appetite control system. The fructose in the apple juice delivers large helpings of fatty acids, while sidestepping the insulin.

That is why we are able to eat more than we really need and our weight keeps relentlessly increasing.

So what really happens when we drink a standard large soft drink? Of the sixty-eight grams of sugar, half is fructose; the thirty-four grams of fructose is converted to fifteen grams of body fat, and our bodies only count half the calories (139). The other 139 calories are completely ignored, which gives our body permission to eat 139 more calories that we would not have otherwise wanted. In the 1900s, our forefathers did not crave so much food because fructose was unheard of in their diet. So the bottom line is, all these extra calories end up on our waistline.

A far saner approach is to not consume the fructose in the first place. You will find that the first thing to disappear, when you stop eating fructose, is lethargy. Exercise will start to make real inroads, as you will not be battling the calories from the fructose intake, and you will have more control over your appetite. The key point is, if you eliminate fructose from your diet, your body will accurately count every calorie. Note: If food tastes sweet, it probably contains fructose; the sweeter the food tastes, the more fructose it contains.

Rules to Go By

If you are thirsty, drink water. Soft drinks are about 6 percent fructose by weight; that becomes ten grams of body fat, for the average can of soft drink. Remember: Apple juice is about 7 percent fructose in weight. That creates about twelve grams of body fat. If you can't face up to water, try drinking sparkling mineral water, but without flavouring, or plain soda water. Pre-packaged ice tea or iced coffee drinks should be avoided, as they are both very high in fructose.

Research has shown that fibre acts to increase the effect of insulin in clearing the blood of the fatty acids caused by fructose. Apples are good because the fibre they contain means you are not left with circulating fatty acids that increase the risk of cardiovascular disease, diabetes, or cancer.

Do not snack on biscuits, as they are very high in sugar and fat. Each cream biscuit contains about three teaspoons (fourteen grams) of sugar; if you eat two of these each day, you are consuming six grams of undetected fatty acids, which goes directly into your arteries. If you had four cream biscuits a day, maybe two for morning tea and two for afternoon tea, that is 420 calories and 28 grams of fructose; that equates to dumping 12.5 grams of fat into your arteries. The amazing thing is, however, that the appetite control system (hypothalamus) would have only counted 308 calories. It takes nine thousand calories to put one kilogram of fat on a person.

Why Do Most Diets Fail?

Where most diets fail is, when people stop their diet, they go back to their old habits and so return to eating fructose and again make the same mistake of overriding the appetite control mechanism, so with no appetite control, they consequently return to gaining weight.

Trans fat is a type of unsaturated fat, and like fructose, it has been in our diet in significant quantities in the last forty years. Vegetable oil used for deep frying should be avoided, as it contains up to 45 percent of trans fats. Remember: When you heat olive oil, it becomes toxic. It has been proven that trans fats increase LDL (bad) cholesterol and consequently increases the risk of heart disease.

Whenever your body comes off something it is dependent on, the body reacts and this causes withdrawal symptoms, it may show up differently in different people, but we all get them. If you can get through the two-week withdrawal period, from there on, everything will become dramatically easier. When fructose is removed from your diet, your food cravings will stop. Take heart: You did not gain weight overnight, and you will not lose it overnight either, but by avoiding sugary drinks and snacks, you will barely notice the change in your diet.

We are now going to look at a healthy, effective, Godly lifestyle.

The first step is that without peace in your life, all the exercises and diets are not going to mean anything. We know that if the illness is not caused by stress, then it is certainly made worse by it. When it comes to stress, we have two choices: We can change the situation or learn to be content with whatever the circumstances, as stated in Philippians 4:11.

In reality, you must have a loving walk with God in order to have good health in every area of your life. This is brought out in 3 John

2 (NKJV): "Beloved, I pray that you may prosper in all things and be in health, just as your soul prospers." Make it a priority to have daily quiet time with God with no interruptions (TV or phone).

Jesus got up before dawn and went to a solitary place to pray. Remember: God looks on your heart and not your surroundings; take time, wait, and hear God answer. Remember: Prayer time calms the nerves and relieves stress; it heads off problems before they arise. Praising God invites His presence into our lives, and His presence comes to transform us and our circumstances.

Note: His compassion never fails; it is new every morning:

"Through the LORD's mercies we are not consumed, because His compassions fail not.

They are new every morning; great is Your faithfulness" (Lamentations 3:22–23 NKJV).

"Pleasant words are like a honeycomb, sweetness to the soul and health to the bones" (Proverbs 16:24 NKJV).

Your peaceful lifestyle will come from what you enjoy doing the most; with the overflow, you will bless others from what has already blessed you. A further scripture to remember is a heart at peace gives life to the body: "A sound heart is life to the body" (Proverbs 14:30 NKJV).

From God's point of view, the main reason for losing weight is to have a long, healthy life of service for His kingdom; fitting into your clothes is not motivation enough.

Here are some helpful hints:

- When choosing food, ask yourself, is this man-made or God-made? How pure can I get it?

- The fewer items in a meal, the less you are tempted to overeat, and the easier it is to digest.
- Do not eat overcooked or processed foods.
- Drink water, herbal teas, and freshly squeezed juices.
- Do not eat fried food.
- Chew your food well.
- 50 percent of every meal should consist of either fruit or raw or cooked vegetables.

To live a life free of the effects of stress and keep in touch with your creator, you should do the following:

- Have regular times of fasting and prayer.
- Flush your body free from impurities by drinking pure water (eight glasses per day or 2 litres).
- Exercise daily; it also helps in getting a deep peaceful rest at night.

Research has shown that these three things shorten people's lives:

- too much stress
- poor eating habits
- lack of exercise

There are three main benefits of exercise:

- It eliminates poisons.
- It increases circulation.
- It strengthens muscles.

The pay-off is, the more oxygen you get into your body, the purer the bloodstream becomes. The main benefit to the heart is, when you are physically fit, the heart does not have to beat as hard and fast as when you are out of shape, so do not sit around too much watching TV and eating snacks. It has also been found that 75 percent of people with chronic back problems do not exercise (and have not exercised for years). We now know that not only will you live longer if you exercise regularly, but you will also have a better quality of life.

Do not say that you are going to exercise when you feel like it; that will not happen. You need to schedule an exercise program at least three time a week, for a minimum of thirty minutes each session. It is definitely worth the effort to get up early and exercise because you are fresher in the morning. Always remember to take five minutes to warm up before you do anything strenuous. One of the best ways to wake up your body is to drink two glasses of water and spend time in reading and prayer, and then start on warm-up exercise such as jogging on the spot.

If you are stiff and sore after exercising, do not give up on it. Keep to your regular schedule; it only takes two days for the soreness to go away. Make sure that you stop eating one hour before exercise.

Why do overweight people breathe heavily? Because their normal-sized lungs cannot get oxygen to all the extra fat cells. Your lung size does not increase with your body size. What causes the sharp pain or stitch in your side? Doctors say it is a cramp in the diaphragm that happens because of waste build-up due to inadequate oxygenation; that simply means the blood does not inhale oxygen and exhale carbon dioxide fast enough. The best thing to do for a stitch is to stop exercising and breath slowly and deeply until it stops.

Note: If you go on quick weight loss diets, you lose water and muscle, and later regain the weight plus extra fat. You must exercise and eat properly as a lifestyle; don't go on a starvation diet because your metabolism will slow down to counteract the lack of calories and so the diet will not benefit you. Always remember that when you exercise, muscles build up and fat burns. You do not have to be concerned with your inner thighs, buttocks, stomach, or hips; just be concerned with exercising the whole body properly, and all the excess fat will eventually be removed. The older we get, the less we need to eat and the more we need to exercise because our metabolism slows down.

There are many good reasons why we should exercise:

- It helps you lose weight and keep it off.
- It strengthens your heart muscles.
- It increases your endurance.
- It improves your quality of sleep.
- It lifts your spirits and makes you feel better.
- It makes you less susceptible to disease.
- It improves your complexion.
- It reduces tension.
- It enables you to handle stress more effectively.
- It relieves depression.
- It causes your nervous system to function more effectively.
- It eases your heart's work load by causing your muscles to use oxygen more efficiently.
- It increases self-esteem, confidence, and a feeling of self-worth.
- It relieves tension headaches.
- It aids the digestive process.
- It slows down the aging process.
- It relieves arthritis.
- It eliminates chronic fatigue.
- It improves your circulation.
- It helps regulate an out-of-control appetite.

The Bible sums up perfectly the reason to look after your body:

"Or do you not know that your body is the temple of the Holy Spirit who is in you, whom you have from God, and you are not your own?

For you were bought at a price; therefore, glorify God in your body and in your spirit, which are God's" (1 Corinthians 6:19–20 NKJV).

Fasting is a discipline that God has designed to bring us into a greater knowledge of Him, to release us into more fullness and power of the Holy Spirit's work in our lives, and to bring us into better health.

Note: Many people fast but have no religious beliefs. They want a natural cure or cleansing for the body. For Christians, fasting is a divine connection to the pride of the human heart. Although it is a discipline to the body, it has a tendency to humble the soul.

Here are some good reasons to fast:

- to receive divine guidance, revelation, or an answer to a specific problem
- to cope with present monumental difficulties
- to break through depression
- to seek the Lord when he is directing you to do something you don't think you can do
- to be set free from everyday sins like pride, jealousy, resentment, gluttony, and gossiping
- to hear God better and have better understanding of His will

Key point: The day before you start your fast, you should eat only fruit and vegetables to cleanse your body, and again when you break your fast, only eat fruit and vegetables on the first day.

How to Get Perfect Rest God's Way

You are on your way to a victorious life when you are totally at peace in every aspect of your life, when you have brought everything to the Lord daily; when you only eat food the way God made it; when you have had plenty of exercise, fresh air, and water; and when you have fasted.

Daniel's Diet

Now we are going to have an in-depth look at Daniel's Diet, which is very popular with Christians. This is named after the young Hebrew slave who was taken captive from Jerusalem and brought to Babylon in 605 BC; this was under the rule of King Nebuchadnezzar. The Babylonian overseer stated that he had to eat the king's finest meats, delicacies, and wines or else he would be killed.

Daniel was so sure of God's principles for health that he replied, "Please test your servants for ten days and let us be given some vegetables to eat and water to drink. Then let our appearance be observed in your presence, and the appearance of the youths who are eating the King's choice food and deal with your servants according to what you see" (Daniel 1:12–13 NLT).

The proof was given in Daniel 1:15–16 (NKJV):

"And at the end of ten days their features appeared better and fatter in flesh than all the young men who ate the portion of the king's delicacies,

Thus, the steward took away their portion of delicacies and the wine that they were to drink, and gave them vegetables."

Key point: In these days of quick fix solutions like take-away or fast foods, the fastest option does not mean the best option; most people do not really know what pre-packaged processed foods are doing to their body. We have previously seen how bad high-fructose corn syrup is, and now we have to put up with taste enhancers such as MSG, which really perverts the taste buds. Manufacturers are motivated by profit and not the consumer's health and well-being. Research has shown that what we do and do not put into our mouths causes a lot of our ill health. We have to start detoxifying our body and overcome the cravings of these harmful and addictive foods.

The result of our Western eating habits is that over 80 percent of the population suffer in varying degrees from sickness and tiredness. For example, we take in our fruit incorrectly: We juice it, such as orange juice, and that makes it very acidic. It goes through the liver, whereas eating the whole orange with the fibre, goes through the intestines.

We saw previously that mankind is a triune being, so we really have to look at the connection among the spirit, soul (mind, will, and emotions), and body. You may be surprised that stress and negative emotions release harmful toxins inside your body. Fear, for example, triggers more than fourteen hundred known physical and chemical reactions, and activates more than thirty different hormones and neurotransmitters. It is not surprising, then, that the Bible mentions "fear not" 365 times; that is equal to once per day for the year. If that is not bad enough, we have to put up with pesticides and chemicals on our food; that is why Merilyn and I have an aquaponics system and grow our own fish and vegetables. Merilyn's favourite saying is, "Eat fresh, grow your own."

It may surprise you that 70 percent of the average person's diet consists of nonessential food. This is quite disturbing, when it only takes 25 percent of nonessential food to cause health problems. Toxins, chemicals, and foreign substances inexorably build up in our bodies to a level beyond what we can naturally eliminate on a daily basis. The body does not know the best way to handle this and stores them up in our fat cells; it's the last line of protection. The problem is that fat around the waist means fat around the heart. As we have said before, our health depends on pure circulation of the blood; this greatly depends on what we eat and what we drink.

What Is Detoxification?

Detoxification is simply getting rid of any harmful substances from the body. It is important because it helps us to withstand the daily bombardment of free radicals on our mind and body. This is overcome by a good supply of antioxidants and herbs from your garden. The payoff from regular detoxing is that there is less likelihood of experiencing illnesses and unfavourable side effects due to our modern lifestyle.

The Bible says that we are the temple of the Holy Spirit (1 Corinthians 3:16); we only get one body, so we had better look after it. What are some of the culprits that are injurious to our body?

- emotional stress
- alcohol
- drugs
- cigarettes
- sugar and salt

A couple of solutions would be to use toothpaste and shampoos that don't have sodium lauryl sulphate; you should also avoid mercury and lead fillings (ask your dentist for white or gold fillings). Avoid deodorants that contain aluminium. Use a filter for drinking and cooking water. Avoid using a microwave for cooking food, and finally, eat organic food if possible.

What Are Antioxidants?

Antioxidants are active ingredients found in natural foods; they neutralise and eliminate oxidants (toxins) from our bodies. They hold the balance of power between toxic overload and good health. The Goji berry is known as the king of the antioxidants. The real problem is overeating processed foods because of the depletion of our body's nutrient supply. Why? Because the majority of processed foods do not contain enough of the necessary nutrients.

What are some of the benefits of antioxidants?

- They lower your blood pressure.
- They inhibit the spread of cancer.
- They help to prevent Alzheimer's disease.

Our Internal Filter System

The liver and kidneys are our internal filtration system; the liver processes about two litres of blood every minute. However, if the liver is continually overloaded, it will become blocked, just like any other filter; since we cannot change the filter, we have to get it detoxified. If the liver is not performing properly, it causes fatigue and weakens the immune system. A wonderful blood cleanser is the beetroot. It helps the liver, gall bladder, and kidneys to function better.

Why is Daniel's Diet so effective? Because it gives a quick weight loss plan in the first ten days and then encourages a gradual weight loss afterwards; it is not a yo-yo diet. Another reason is because it is a restricted and cleansing diet. The obvious benefits would be extra energy, good health, and a clear mind.

Why Is Daniel's Diet So Different?

Unlike other diets, it is a partial fast for a set amount of time. A fast requires eating no food, but a partial fast allows an unlimited (with wisdom) amounts of specified food. Its main purpose is to lose weight and to detoxify the body. It will also give you control over your eating.

People joke about love handles, but they are not cute; they are toxic waste dumps. Gooey fat cells are like small sticky bubbles clumping together around your thighs, heart, and stomach. Try to imagine this: Every time you eat sugar, chocolate, refined carbohydrates, deep fried foods, and junk food, these fat cells multiply.

It is worth repeating: Drink plenty of water. Why? Because it reduces and dissolves fat cells and flushes them back into the body's elimination system; by exercising at the same time, the body is able to burn up the released fat as energy. Regular bowel movements will avoid toxic build-up in the colon and prevent colon cancer.

How Does Constipation Affect the Body?

Constipation causes the following:

* headaches
* irritability
* tiredness
* skin problems
* poor concentration

So what is the natural solution? It is certainly not taking laxatives; they are only good for the short term. The natural solution is eating natural foods containing fibre and drinking eight glasses of water per day. Research has shown that people who have unfinished issues in their lives are often constipated; this automatically improves when the situation has been dealt with. What is the solution to constipation? The key is to eat slowly and to thoroughly chew your food. The appetite control system is then satisfied and sends this signal to the brain: "Stop eating, I am full." What happens in reality is, it takes twenty minutes or more for the brain to receive a not-hungry signal from the stomach. So if we scoff down our meal in ten minutes, it will actually take ten more minutes before we feel satisfied, so because we still feel hungry, we keep on eating.

What Is Comfort Eating?

Comfort eating is really a form of co-dependency or escapism; in reality, it is a tranquiliser. If the underlying issue that triggers the desire for more food is not addressed, then this desire for comfort food will continue. Using food as a tranquiliser only masks the problem, so you have short-term comfort, but still have a long-term problem.

How Does Food Actually Tranquilise?

Blood sugar levels rise with sugary food. Eating these foods stimulates different endorphins in the brain, which has the effect of natural painkillers, relaxants, and pleasure stimulations; they manipulate the brain's biochemistry to cause the body to feel satisfied, happy, fulfilled, and relaxed. A lot of foods can cause this sensation, but sugar and chocolate are on the top of the list.

Unfortunately, comfort eating can snare anyone into an endless cycle of escapism, overeating, and depression; like all drugs, you need to have more and more to avoid the endorphins dropping. The bottom line is, people can easily become emotionally dependant on food, to cope with everyday life. The solution to this dilemma is accepting that no food, drug, or stimulant can ever fulfil your heart's desire; it only masks the issue, which needs to be dealt with on its own merit.

Breaking off Addictions

The Bible has the answer to breaking off addictions, and it is found in Romans 12:2(NKJV): "And do not be conformed to this world, but be transformed by the renewing of your mind, that you may prove what is that good and acceptable and perfect will of God."

So do not underestimate the power of prayer and faith in the healing process. Research has shown that prayer raises the body's natural immunity quite significantly, as well as forming a relationship with God. This is brought out in James 5:16 (NKJV): "Confess your trespasses to one another, and pray for one another, that you may be healed. The effective, fervent prayer of a righteous man avails much."

The Power of Your Words

The key to this is to change your self-talk; you need to change negative thoughts like these:

- I'm unlucky.
- I'm fat.
- I can't do this diet.
- Nobody likes me.
- I'm lonely.
- I'll never lose this weight.
- I'll never change.
- God never answers my prayers.
- I'm too old to change.

If you keep making these statements, you will start to believe them, and this will affect your spirit, emotions, and body. The answer is, you must replace these negative statements with positive statements and speak God's word over yourself. Try to replace bad habits with prayer and reading the Bible, combined with exercise.

Wonderfully Designed Brain

The quality of our food determines whether our brain performs properly or not. Remember: Nutrition is actually fuel. If a car's fuel is dirty, it will not run properly, and neither will we. Poor quality nutrition will cause disruption of the brain signals and normal functions. Our mind is not the only thing affected; our emotions and attitudes and even our temperament is as well. Amazingly, our brain contains ten billion nerve cells, called neurons. Chemicals released in the brain are called neurotransmitters; these control our mood, memory, appetite, sleep patterns, sex drive, and our ability to learn. Our brain fuel needs to be composed of vitamins, minerals, amino acids, glucose, and enzymes to make this wonderfully designed, complex organ function as it was designed.

What Keeps the Brain from Working Properly?

- lack of water
- lack of sleep
- lack of nutrients
- sugar
- stress

What Causes Migraine Headache?

Research has also shown that at least two-thirds of migraines are caused by allergic reactions to foods. Chocolate is high on the list, followed by sugar and dairy products. People suffering from headaches should take the time to wean themselves off chocolate, caffeine, sugar, and orange juice, before starting a Daniel Diet.

What Are the Symptoms of Caffeine Overload?

- irritability
- insomnia
- nervousness
- headaches
- anxiety
- raised blood pressure
- heart palpitations and trembling
- restlessness

A very popular drink in Western culture is coffee with milk and sugar. This combination is really a lethal cocktail, but most of us are oblivious to it.

Note: People suffering from any heart problems, nervous disorders, high blood pressure, depression, irritable bowel, or lethargy, and all those who are pregnant or planning a baby, should avoid caffeine entirely. Green tea, however, contains powerful antioxidants that are beneficial in fighting free radical toxins, cancer, and cholesterol. It has been shown that green tea also helps to restore energy; it controls blood pressure and is beneficial in combating diabetes.

What Exactly Is Margarine?

Most people do not know that nearly all margarines are artificially coloured and flavoured; they also contain stabilisers. Manufacturers do this to make it solid and easy to spread and to increase its shelf life, but in reality, it is very close to being plastic. Margarine includes substances called trans fatty acids. They act like saturated fats in our body, and unknown to most people, they stimulate the production of cholesterol. This fatty acid is *not* natural; it has no natural metabolic function, and consequently, the body does not have the capacity to handle it. Research has shown that it contributes to the creation of gallstones and heart disease.

What is the answer? Organic butter is better and healthier than traditional margarines. Daniel's Diet does not include butter, but it is alright to use olive oil as a dressing on your salads.

The source of our problem is our modern farming methods, which push our soils to the limit with superphosphates, pesticides, and herbicides. This eventually leads to digestive overload and food allergies. Another problem is the overcooking and refining of grains, which destroy the natural enzymes needed for proper digestion and assimilation. This causes toxic overload and can damage your intestines.

What Do They Do to Bread?

Most people do not know that chemicals are used in our refining and milling methods; bleaching agents are used to make bread nice and white. Wheat grain is not naturally white in colour; it is golden brown. If you have any of the following symptoms, you should give up eating white bread immediately:

- headaches
- lethargy
- bloating
- constipation

Dairy Products

What happens when people come off dairy products? Here are some of the documented results:

- increased energy
- weight loss
- disappearance of mucus problems
- no more constipation
- decrease in stomach problems and arthritis

Dairy products cause the following aliments in children:

- stomach problems
- unhappiness
- skin complaints
- frequent vomiting
- frequent crying

You may say, "But milk contains calcium." Yes, but it is not easy to digest. The problem is, when we become adults, we lose our ability to make the enzyme lactase, which is needed to digest lactose, and consequently, this is what creates lactose intolerance.

So where can we get our calcium from? People get enough calcium from their diet of fresh fruit and vegetables (all green leafy vegetables contain calcium). Fish and free-range eggs are all high in calcium.

Sugar: A Slow Poison

Sugar has been referred to as "white death"; in using it, we are slowly poisoning ourselves. Diabetes, which is now an epidemic in our society, is just one manifestation of excess sugar. Unfortunately, sugar is included in most of our packaged, tinned, and mixed foods. It is worth mentioning again: Sugar causes depletion of blood glucose, and this is certainly not good for the proper functioning of the brain. The bottom line is, sugar is quickly absorbed into our bloodstream, which causes excess insulin to be released from the pancreas. This excess sugar is converted into triglycerides, which causes a storage of fat. The problem is exacerbated because in consuming empty calories, your body craves more to eat because of the lack of nutrients.

Here are some problems of sugar-related symptoms:

- nervousness, irritability, and exhaustion
- muscle and joint pains
- Type 2 diabetes
- dizziness and tremors
- forgetfulness, anxiety, aggression, and mood swings
- obesity
- headaches and migraines
- skin problems
- eyesight problems
- poor immunity

Research has shown the following problems with sugar in children because they are eating more soft drinks, cakes, and chocolate bars than our forefathers:

- poor concentration
- tiredness
- tooth decay
- diabetes
- obesity
- acne
- recurring sickness

Looking back to the bygone era, our forefathers mainly ate fruit, grains, and natural honey; they also ate raw nuts (not roasted), which were already unrefined carbohydrates and so were consequently broken down into simple sugars. Therefore, avoid the problems associated with refined sugar. Even the Bible says not to eat too much honey, as it may make you vomit.

"Have you found honey? Eat only as much as you need, lest you be filled with it and vomit" (Proverbs 25:16 NKJV).

White Sugar Makes Us Tired and Dull Minded

Refined sugar enters the bloodstream too quickly. This rush gives us an instant energy surge; it is often referred to as a sugar rush. Yes, there is an initial burst of energy, but it is unnatural and quickly dissipates. The problem is, once the extra supply of insulin has combatted the sugar in the blood, it creates a downer. As I mentioned before, this drop in blood sugar is called hypoglycaemia. The answer is not more sweets but eating more wholesome foods.

Balance Is the Key

There is more than enough evidence to prove that eating more vegetables and fruit is the single most important dietary change to maintain good health. The specific ingredients found in fruit, vegetables, and seeds are so powerful that they often win the fight against cancer.

"Biodynamic" means that food is grown in soil naturally and is chemical free; that was how it was in the Garden of Eden. Avoid all food that is genetically engineered; what they are saying is that God needs some help. The Bible says that food was created perfectly according to its own kind. This is shown in Genesis 1:12 (NKJV): "And the earth brought forth grass, the herb that yields seed according to its kind, and the tree that yields fruit, whose seed is in itself according to its kind. And God saw that it was good."

Humanity knows the number of seeds in an apple, but only God know the number of apples in a seed. If God said it was good, then it does not need to be improved on.

The bottom line is, God has a holistic health plan for us. The body and the mind will be looked after by Daniel's Diet, and our spirit will be looked after by our relationship with Jesus Christ through the Holy Spirit.

"So you shall serve the LORD your God, and He will bless your bread and your water. And I will take sickness away from the midst of you" (Exodus 23:25 NKJV).

PART 6

Kingdom Living

This will be the most important subject of the six major segments of this book. By now, you should have absolutely no condemnation about the tithe yet have a greater love and joy to give from the heart. God looks on the inside, but man looks on the outside. Always remember: God won't without us, and we can't without Him.

Key point: Read the whole Bible for inspiration and gratitude, but always remember: Christians now live under the New Covenant, not the Old Covenant.

It is interesting that Jesus spoke about the kingdom of God over a hundred times but mentioned church only twice. Yes, it is joyful to get together with family, friends, and fellow Christians at church, but the emphasis should not be on the property (church buildings). It should be on evangelism, missionary support, and kingdom living. We should look and act like the early Christians in the book of Acts.

Kingdom living is having a personal relationship with the Holy Spirit, who now dwells inside the believer's heart:

"Do you not know that you are the temple of God and that the Spirit of God dwells in you?" (1 Corinthians 3:16 NKJV).

Expect the supernatural realm to be involved in your natural realm. Expect and receive God's ideas, not just good ideas, on how to have a joyful, fulfilling marriage and to have more than enough. You are blessed to be a blessing to family and friends and have enough to support evangelism and missionary work. Love looks like something, people who come into contact with you should see grace in you, that you seem to be in love with somebody; yes, that is very true: You should be in love with the Lord Jesus Christ. Your spouse, family, boyfriend, girlfriend, friends, and neighbours should see the qualities of Jesus in you, and your morals should reflect holy living. We do not love the world; we are not worldly. As your love for Jesus, the wonderful Holy Spirit and awesome wonder of God, grows, the things of this world should go strangely dim.

Since we are going to use the word "kingdom," what does it mean? History has shown that a king ruled over a certain amount of land, and the inhabitants were referred to as his subjects. In the Psalms, it says that "God owns the earth," and in another passage, it states that "He has given it over to man." We really do have a lease on the earth, and when that lease runs out, the Lord will return. The Greek word *"Harpazo"* means "the great snatch": It is when Jesus takes His body (Christians who are living today) to the present heaven. There is eventually going to be "a new heaven and a new earth," as Revelation so wonderfully foretells.

Time Management

The greatest tragedy in life is not death but life without a purpose. Kingdom living will give you that purpose. We become what we spend our time on. Have you spent time with the Holy Spirit, or have you been pursuing your own plans?

Key point: The way you invest your time determines the level of success in God's kingdom.

Think of time as a currency; just as you use money to buy things, use time to purchase life. Success really means getting the best returns on the time invested. No one gets more hours per day than anyone else. Once the day has gone, it has gone forever. Our quality of life is in direct proportion to how we spend our time.

What exactly are our priorities? Priorities are doing the right thing at the right time in the right way. It stops us doing the wrong thing at the wrong time in the wrong way. Priorities also help us to see our progress towards our written goals. Without priorities, time goes sailing by, like a ship without a rudder, and before you know it, ten years have gone by, and nothing much has been achieved. The bottom line is, correct priorities protect you from wasting your time and energy. Always ask yourself, "What is the most effective use of my time right now?" Correct priorities mean God's priorities, and God's priority is kingdom first. This is the fuel that keeps you on track to establish your end goal. Priorities also help to simplify life, in this complex world we live in.

Note: The greatest failure in life is being successful in your own assignment and not doing God's assignment.

Without priorities, we seem to major on trivialities, which result in preoccupation with the unimportant, and the consequences are ineffective activities. Now without focus, people simply misuse their gifts and talents.

Jesus discussed the kingdom living philosophy very succinctly:

"Therefore I say to you, do not worry about your life, what you will eat or what you will drink; nor about your body, what you will put on. Is not life more than food and the body more than clothing?

Look at the birds of the air, for they neither sow nor reap nor gather into barns; yet your heavenly Father feeds them. Are you not of more value than they?

Which of you by worrying can add one cubit to his stature?

So why do you worry about clothing? Consider the lilies of the field, how they grow; They neither toil nor spin;

and yet I say to you that even Solomon in all his glory was not arrayed like one of these.

Now if God so clothes the grass of the field, which today is, and tomorrow is thrown into the oven, will He not much more clothe you, O you of little faith?" (Matthew 6:25–30 NKJV).

Jesus did not say not to plan for tomorrow; He said not to worry about tomorrow. Worry is the most useless exercise in the world. Why? Because it does not change anything for the better; it consumes our energy, our time, our talents, and our gifts, and it even consumes our imagination.

Matthew 6:33 (NKJV) says, "But seek first the kingdom of God and His righteousness, and all these things shall be added to you."

This is achieved by seeking opportunities to introduce others to the kingdom of God.

The word "Lord" means master or owner; we cannot call Him Lord and then do our own thing, without ever asking Him for advice. Either He owns us or He doesn't. If God cannot ask for anything He wants from us at any time without us putting up a fight, then He is not really our Lord. The bottom line is, nothing we give up for the sake of the kingdom is a loss to us. Why? The Lord Jesus gives more to us than we could ever give to Him.

How to Find God

Jeremiah explained how you will find God:

"And you will seek Me and find Me, when you search for Me with all your heart" (Jeremiah 29:13 NKJV).

Finding God is the same as finding His kingdom. Jesus reduced the issues of life to two things: the kingdom of God and the righteousness of God. Everything else is really superfluous. The nations of the world have a constitution, and so does the kingdom of God; it is called the Bible. The kingdom makes you a citizen, but your righteousness, which was bought by the shed blood of Jesus, gives you access to all the rights, resources, and privileges of being a citizen. How do you know you are obeying all the kingdom laws? You know because you are living a holy life. Holiness is not a doctrine; it is a lifestyle.

What are the advantages of living a righteous life? It will prevent the death of your business, your marriage, and your health (Proverbs 11:5).

Righteousness also addresses the big picture in Proverbs 14:34 (NLT): "Godliness makes a nation great, but sin is a disgrace to any people.

Every law that is disobeyed, leads a nation further down the path of disgrace, disillusionment, disintegration and eventually it collapses."

People get short-term gain with unscrupulous practises, but end up with long-term pain. The Bible says this very cogently in Proverbs 16:8 (NLT): "Better to have little with Godliness than to be rich and dishonest."

The benefit of righteousness is explained in Proverbs 21:21 (NLT): "Whoever pursues righteousness and unfailing love will find life, righteousness and honour."

The results of the kingdom of God is actually explained in Romans 14:17 (NKJV): "For the kingdom of God is not eating and drinking, but righteousness and peace and joy in the Holy Spirit."

On reflection, we can say the following:

- Righteousness is the key to abundant kingdom living.
- Holiness is a manifestation of righteousness (right standing with God).
- Righteousness is a solution to poverty.

Key point: Never mistake knowledge for wisdom; one helps you make a living, and the other helps you make a life.

Advertisers all over the world relentlessly tell us that the way to get peace and joy is to get more things, but Jesus said it very succinctly: "...for one's life does not consist in the abundance of the things he possesses." Luke 12.15b (NKJV)

Is your hunger for the kingdom of God greater than your hunger for possessions and things? Jesus also said, in Matthew 5:6 (NKJV), "Blessed are those who hunger and thirst for righteousness, for they shall be filled."

If this kingdom lifestyle is your chief desire and delight, God will take care of everything else.

Psalm 37:4 (NKJV) says, "Delight yourself also in the LORD, and He shall give you the desires of your heart."

Does Righteousness Have Any Fruit?

Yes, generosity is a character trait of the righteous. Some even go on to be patrons of the gospel; their whole purpose is to fund the gospel. Jesus said it is more blessed to give than to receive.

Always remember: It is the motive behind your giving, and not the amount that you give, that God sees.

The bottom line is, the destiny and prosperity of the ancient Israelites were inexorably connected to the land. If you want to leave your children and grandchildren a legacy, leave them land.

The payoff is that if we are righteous, we will enjoy the fruit of peace because we are not chasing after things anymore. But this peace can also give you a calm disposition when in trouble. God gave Merilyn and I a supernatural peace and confidence when we were lost in the National Forest for a whole day, before three men in a four-wheel drive came and rescued us. The peace was so heavy on us, we couldn't have worried if we had have tried.

Key point: Unlike religion, which focuses on the outside appearance, life in the kingdom of God focuses on inner transformation, which manifests itself in external ways. Always remember that man looks on the outside, but God looks on the inside.

Religion has proven itself to be a great divider of mankind, but the kingdom of God should unite us. The word of God says, "Where there is unity God commands the blessing." The Hebrew word "*mamlakah*," which means "dominion," can also be translated as "kingdom." In essence, mankind was created to have rulership over the earth. When Adam and Eve fell from grace, they lost a kingdom, not a religion. No religion in the world can take the place of the kingdom of God or fill the vacuum in his soul. The hunger of the human heart is for the lost kingdom. The heart of the problem is the problem of the human heart.

Note: Everything Jesus said and did—His teachings, healings, and miracles—were focused on a kingdom, not on a religion. The bottom line is, Jesus had only one message, one mission, one mandate: the return of the kingdom of heaven to earth.

Let's look at the difference between religion and the kingdom of God:

- Religion focuses on heaven; the kingdom focuses on earth.
- Religion wants to escape the earth; the kingdom influences and changes the earth.
- Religion seeks to take earth to heaven; the kingdom seeks to bring heaven to earth.
- Religion prepares man to leave the earth; the kingdom enables man to dominate the earth.

Jesus said in Matthew 15:6b (NKJV), "You have made the commandment of God of no effect by your tradition."

This promise is in Matthew 6:33 (NKJV): "But seek first the kingdom of God and His righteousness, and all these things shall be added to you." This includes all your physical, social, emotional, and financial needs that promote a sense of self-worth and purpose.

Who makes God to be King and Lord? Nobody! He is King and Lord because He is the creator. He takes personal responsibility for us, not as His servants but as His family. An earthly king should look after the needs of his citizens, so our heavenly King will look after His children. Therefore, when we submit to King Jesus, we come under His provision; He cares for, looks after, and protects us. No human government has effectively taken care of its poor; that is why the kingdom of God, taught by Jesus, is superior to all human systems, which are weak and full of loopholes. Just remember: 90 percent of all national and international problems are the result of either governments, or religions, or both.

Deep down, we are all searching for a kingdom where we are all equal. We all want the same rights, recognition, security, and health; we want to live our lives with meaning and purpose. The wonderful thing is that sharing the kingdom of God will bring fulfilment, joy, and purpose.

Definition of the Kingdom of God

Simply stated, a kingdom is a domain over which a king has rulership. This means he governs over entities, territories, and human beings. Because God rules over sickness, poverty, and oppression, we can get supernatural help to fight this fallen world. We are all searching for this illusive kingdom, but without God, we will not find it.

On reflection, as citizens of heaven, we inhabit the earth to influence it with the culture and values of heaven, to bring it under kingdom rule; further, the kingdom of heaven wants sons and daughters and not just servants.

Let's look at some scriptures to show that Jesus was clearly kingdom minded:

"Our Father in heaven, hallowed be Your name.

Your kingdom come. Your will be done on earth as it is in heaven" (Matthew 6:9b–10 NKJV).

Matthew 24:14 (NKJV) says, "And this gospel of the kingdom will be preached in all the world as a witness to all the nations, and then the end will come."

Note: Any conscientious king would want his citizens to be happy, prosperous, and content. This is summed up succinctly in 3 John 2 (NKJV): "Beloved, I pray that you may prosper in all things and be in health, just as your soul prospers."

On reflection, a king can give or distribute anything to anyone in his kingdom. If we obey King Jesus, we show that we believe that He owns everything and that not only can He replace what we give, He can even multiply it.

The word says, "Where there is unity, God commands a blessing," so believers joining together can dispel the spiritual darkness wherever they go. The kingdom is not just in word only but in power and in the Holy Spirit and in much assurance:

"For our gospel did not come to you in word only, but also in power, and in the Holy Spirit and in much assurance, as you know what kind of men we were among you for your sake" (1 Thessalonians 1:5 NKJV).

Unfortunately, there are many preachers today who only have a mental knowledge of the kingdom and not an experiential knowledge; they have never witnessed healings or casting out demons. The bottom line is, righteousness, peace, and joy are only really possible when the Holy Spirit moves us.

Jesus gave us one of the keys in Matthew 11:12 (NKJV): "And from the days of John the Baptist until now the kingdom of heaven suffers violence, and the violent take it by force."

So when we pray, we can pull down to earth whatever is in heaven (that is, health, peace, joy, forgiveness, miracles, healing, and prosperity). Sickness does not exist in heaven, so the power from heaven can be manifested, and people can be healed and set free in the name of Jesus. The supernatural realm now touches the natural realm. In reality, every decision you make must be based on kingdom principles and commandments.

Key point: God wants His kingdom to manifest in you. He wants His realm to spread to others through you, bringing righteousness, peace, and joy in the Holy Spirit. The pay-off is that we do not have to be dominated and controlled by circumstances, problems, and Satan.

Here are four ways to show that man is really like his creator:

1. God is spirit, and the core of humanity is spirit.

2. God thinks and imagines and generates ideas and plans, and human beings do the same.
3. God expresses emotion, and so do human beings.
4. God experiences pain when He is rejected, and so do we.

In His kingdom, you cannot go wrong if you do what Jesus did, so really, to be supernatural means to act like Jesus. 1 John 4:17 (NKJV) says, "Love has been perfected among us in this: that we may have boldness in the day of judgment; because as He is, so are we in this world."

The underlying problem is, some people cannot subdue or bind sickness because it has become so normal to them in everyday life. So in reality, they have given the keys of their health to the enemy. We will know that the kingdom has arrived among us when we see demons being cast out by the Spirit of God.

Why is the kingdom of God different from other religions? If Christ had not been resurrected, it would have been a declaration that death had defeated Him, and He would have been no different from any other philosopher, teacher, or religious leader who had ever lived. We can now walk in resurrection power because of what Jesus did; as the Bible says, "Death, where is your sting; grave, where is your victory?" We simply need to prove the resurrection of Jesus through the supernatural power of the kingdom of God. The bottom line is, His resurrection guarantees our resurrection.

Note: We do not merely have doctrines, theologies, or ceremonies; we have the kingdom of glorious power. Most people have heard what religion says, but they have not heard what the kingdom of God says; they only get a little truth.

All prophets of other religions are in the grave, but the tomb of Jesus is still empty because He sits at the right hand of the Father in heaven. Under this New Covenant, Jesus is our mediator and our intercessor.

1 Timothy 2:5 (NKJV) says, "For there is one God and one Mediator between God and men, the Man Christ Jesus."

The Old Covenant had Moses, but the New Covenant has Jesus. The power of God cannot be manifested until we stop relying on our own abilities. We must die to the old way of life, to obtain the new way of life.

Galatians 2:20 (NKJV) says, "I have been crucified with Christ; it is no longer I who live, but Christ lives in me; and the life which I now live in the flesh I live by faith in the Son of God, who loved me and gave Himself for me."

The more completely you die to self, the more the power of the resurrection will manifest in and through you. The instant Christ was raised from the dead, everything became a possibility to those who believed.

The difference between the kingdom of God and other religions is that religions lack the supernatural power to deal with sin and the transformation of lives; there is no power to heal sickness or to deliver from mental or emotional oppression. So in reality, we don't just know about God; we actually know Him as our Saviour, friend, healer, and deliverer.

In this kingdom, God writes His word not on stone tablets, but on our hearts, so that we may love with His love. So genuine and lasting change can only be found in Jesus Christ. Everyone will know God from the least to the greatest; it is not just for the highly intelligent and educated but for everyone who has a heartbeat.

The amazing fact in this kingdom is that the same Spirit that raised Jesus from the dead lives in every believer, and He wants to manifest Himself to others. We must be aware that the Holy Spirit that dwells within us can be used in any situation, at any time of the day, and His presence in us can be called on in every time of need. Jesus did not give His all so we would do nothing. Our love for God is measured by our love for other people. The reason that this kingdom is different is because law *requires* us to do things and grace *enables* us to do things.

In this kingdom of God, miracles are outside the senses or natural realm of knowledge; science cannot explain it. There is, however, a second type of knowledge, and that is spiritual or revelation knowledge.

When we get to heaven, we will find things are not learned, just simply revealed or known. We get a taste of this on earth through the word of knowledge, the word of wisdom, and the discerning of spirits. Always remember that common sense and logic come from the mind, and revelation comes from the spirit.

What are the consequences of a lack of revealed knowledge? For example, you may not have a vision for your life. Hosea 4:6 (NKJV) says, "My people are destroyed for lack of knowledge. Because you have rejected knowledge, I also will reject you from being a priest for Me; because you have forgotten the law of your God, I also will forget your children."

This is not just intellectual knowledge but God-revealed knowledge in the New Covenant; we all live under these laws, which are now written into our heart. The bottom line is, the enemy will destroy you in any area where you lack relevant knowledge.

So what is the purpose of revelation? It is to challenge people to change and grow, to rise to new levels, to reach new goals, to win back territory that has been held by the enemy, and to subsequently expand the kingdom of God.

Key point: Religion appeals to the carnal man, but the kingdom of God transforms the heart. Always remember that God does not dwell in buildings of cement or brick, but He dwells in us:

"Do you not know that you are the temple of God and that the Spirit of God dwells in you?" (1 Corinthians 3:16 NKJV).

Doctrine in itself does not produce revivals but is caused by people who tap into the spiritual realm, through revelation knowledge that is produced by the Holy Spirit. You could say that doctrine is really the milk of the word, and revelation is the meat of the word. Examples of this would be going from church to kingdom, from old wine to new wine, from theory to experience, from theology to demonstration.

When the Apostle Paul was in Athens, he tried to win the philosophers by intellectual arguments but won very few. He then went later to Corinth and won thousands by signs and wonders (1 Corinthians 2:4).

Key point: Whenever you study the history of the church, when a truth based in scripture was revealed for the first time, it was often classified as false. Kingdom of God people are not old wine people full of theories without supernatural demonstrations.

Note: You must bring your experiences up to God's word, not bring God's word down to your experiences. Always remember: It is easy to preach or teach something that we do not have to prove. Now here is an oxymoron: God is omnipresent, but He only manifests Himself where He is worshiped in spirit and in truth, and where revelation is revealed, it is received by faith.

The bottom line is, a born-again Christian can expect a *rhema* word: a word from God that speaks to the present circumstances and will never contradict the written word of God. In this kingdom, once we have experienced the presence of God, we will not be able to live without it; taste and see that the Lord is good. This will really become a reality.

We should always remember that receiving truths from preachers does not depend on their eloquence but on the condition of the hearts of the people who are hearing them. We study the Bible, not just to learn more about its contents, but to get to know the author, to become more Christ-like.

Key point: Really desire the presence of God, and He will manifest Himself to you.

Always remember: One of the greatest tragedies in life is to become lukewarm and to lose the presence of God and not even be aware of it. When you cease to be changed, you lose your power and go back to religion and formality. To start on the Christian road, we need to be born again; we go from faith to faith, from glory to glory, from victory to victory until we are transformed into the very image of Christ.

Remember: The world will conform you, but the word will transform you: "And do not be conformed to this world but be transformed by the renewing of your mind, that you may prove what is that good and acceptable and perfect will of God" (Romans 12:2 NKJV).

We see that movements come and go, but only the outpouring of the Holy Spirit will transform society. The bottom line is, what changes us is not the time spent in church but the time spent in God's presence: having a quiet time alone with our creator. As our degree of revelation increases, so does the level of our faith.

Merilyn let our son Paul go to church camp when he was about eight years old, and because he seemed to be accident prone, she frequently prayed for him. When they arrived home, the youth pastor told her of their experience: It had been raining, and so the ground was still muddy and slippery on the track where they were walking beside a river. Paul had stopped to get a drink at a drinking fountain, and as he was leaning forward, his feet went from under him, and he began sliding towards the river. The youth pastor was not close enough to stop him from going into the river, so he jumped in so he could catch him. It was springtime, and the water was very cold; the youth pastor was getting washed down the river, but Paul's clothes got caught on a twig, so he was sitting nice and dry on the river bank. The pastor told Merilyn he couldn't believe how it all unfolded like that, until she said that she had been praying protection Paul since before he left for the camp. When you get a revelation of who God is and how much He loves you and your children, it is safe to let your children go out under supervision of someone you trust and know that God will watch over them and protect them, no matter what happens.

We love to sing praises and worship our God, so what is the difference between praise and worship?

Praise is declaring how awesome He is. We sing His praises.

Worship is something that you do, a sincere attitude of humility and reverence and admiration towards God; it is something you devote most of your time to. It consumes your thoughts and attention. It is what you do with your life.

Praise focuses on proclaiming the works of God, but worship focuses on the person of God.

Praise increases the anointing, but worship brings the glory.

Sincere praise breaks demonic strongholds.

Praise and worship songs must be based on God's word and not on tradition. When we sing God's word, He releases His power and anointing. God inhabits the praises of His people.

How can we be an effective witness for Jesus?

- Be filled with the power of the Holy Spirit.
- Give your time to God and be passionate towards Him.
- Love not the world.
- Be able to explain the hope that is within you by knowing His word.

How does one get into the kingdom of God? The answer is in Romans 10:9–10 (NKJV):

"That if you confess with your mouth, the Lord Jesus and believe in your heart that God has raised Him from the dead, you will be saved.

For with the heart one believes unto righteousness, and with the mouth confession is made unto salvation."

After you say the following prayer, ask Jesus to help you always to demonstrate your faith through love; your number one desire should be for God to be glorified in and through you.

Please say this prayer aloud and from your heart:

Lord God, I believe that Jesus Christ is Your Son and that He went to the cross, suffered, and died for my sin. I ask you to forgive me for all my sin and to fill me with Your righteousness. I ask You to be Lord of my life. I thank you that my name is written in the Lamb's Book of Life, that I now have salvation through the precious blood of Jesus, to live for an eternity with You in heaven.

I believe according to Your word that I am now born again. Thank you, Jesus. Amen.

REFERENCES

Part 1. The Old Covenant

1. McVey S. 52 Lies Heard in Church Every Sunday
2. Narramore M. Tithing: Low-Realm, Obsolete, and Defunct
3. Pawson D. Unlocking the Bible
4. Prince D. Blessing or Curse: You can Choose
5. Sapp R. The Children Are Free

Part 2. Grace: The New Covenant

1. Anderson N., Miller R. & Travis P. Grace that Breaks the Chains
2. Davies G. Genius, Grief, and Grace,
3. Godwin R. & Roberts D. The Grace Outpouring
4. Lucado M. Grace Happens Here
5. Prince D. Blessing or Curse: You Can Choose
6. Prince J. Destined to Reign
7. Spurgeon C. All of Grace
8. Stanley A. The Grace of God
9. Strobel L. The case For Grace
10. Swindoll C. The Grace Awakening
11. Wiersbe W. The Bible Exposition Commentary
12. Wommack A. Grace in the Gospels
13. Wommack A Balance of Faith and Grace

Part 3. The Global Financial System

1. Bates L. The New Economic Disorder
2. Bonner W. & Wiggin A. Empire of Debt
3. Das S. Extreme Money
4. Ferguson A. When Money Dies
5. Forbes S. Money
6. Grant J. The Forgotten Depression,
7. Gasparino C. The Sellout
8. Griffin G. E. The Creature From Jekyll Island
9. Lowenstein R. The End Of Wall Street
10. Morris C. The Trillion Dollar Melt Down
11. Reich R. Super Capitalism
12. Rickards J. The Death of Money
13. Rickards J. Currency Wars
14. Schiff P. The Real Crash
15. Soros G. The Crash of 2008
16. Stiglitz J. Freefall
17. Stockman D. The Great Deformation
18. Truit and Rabino The Money Bubble

Part 4. Personal Prosperity

1. Brott R and Damazio F. Biblical Principles for Becoming Debt Free
2. Bruning N. Don't Panic
3. Clitheroe P. Making Money
4. Keesee G. Financially Free
5. Ramsay D. The Total Money Makeover

Part 5. Excellent Health

1. Bridgeman P. Daniel's Diet
2. Gillespie D. Sweet Poison Why Sugar Makes You Fat
3. Guarneri M. The Science of Natural Healing

4. Horne R. The Health Revolution
5. Omartian S. Greater Health God's Way
6. Sapolsky R. Stress and Your Body

Part 6. Kingdom Living

1. Hinn B. The Miracle of Healing
2. Johnson B. Experiencing the Impossible
3. Maldonado G. The Kingdom of Power
4. Maldonado G. Supernatural Transformation
5. Maldonado G. Experiencing the glory of God
6. McVey S. 52 Lies Heard in Church Every Sunday
7. Munroe M. Preparing for Kingdom Experience and Expansion
8. Munroe M. Applying The Kingdom
9. Munroe M. Releasing Your Potential
10. Peterson D. Transformed by God

Printed in the United States
By Bookmasters